I0011534

Getting Closer With

LibreOffice Writer

PREFACE

Bismillahirrahmaanirrahim.

      This book aims to be one of resources for people who want to go deep into and get more knowledge in term of LibreOffice Writer. It titled "Getting Closer With LibreOffice Writer" which we dedicate for All Indonesian people. This book has two versions, mobile and ready-to-print version which mobile has … pages and ready-to-print has 225 pages. **This book has been collaboratively written by 1 cover contributor, 6 Language editors, 3 book editors, 15 chapter writers and 12 chapter Translator.**

Change Log

- Coordinator of project Taufik Hidayat <yumtaufik1997@gmail.com> was planning Collaborative book project "Getting Closer With LibreOffice Writer"

- The project was introduced on Belajar GNU/Linux Indonesia Telegram group on 29 June 2016.

- The Collaborative book project was started on 16 July 2016 by Taufik Hidayat <yumtaufik1997@gmail.com> and was officially launched on Belajar GNU/Linux Indonesia Telegram group to invite all members contribute to this project.

- Each chapter in the book was composed systematically based on contributor's submission. This was done to maintain respectful from all contributors.

Objective

The main goal of this project is to serve handy book for beginner especially for those who just started learning Office Suite software in GNU/Linux. Besides, it also promotes Free software to avoid illegal usage of software (worst explanation is "piracy") issues through using Free Software LibreOffice. We believe the issues have significant implication in our belief and personality.

Method

This book has been cooperatively written by all contributor from different region in Indonesia. It has inspired and motivated us to conduct this project continuously.

Deadline

Deadline project was on 30 October 2016.

Expectancy

Through this E-book, People from all region in Indonesia can print ant share it easily with no high cost. We expect this book will inspire other Community-based organization conducting similar collaborative projects. Just imagine, every FOSS-based community in Indonesia conduct the same, it will give enough local resources to educate people in term of "importance of FOSS".

Closure

Finally, we really appreciate all contributor respectively for IRC #ubuntu-indonesia, Inkscape Indonesia community on Facebook, Belajar GNU/Linux Indonesia community on Telegram, collaborative book project contributor and all people which we can not mention it one by one.

We do apologize to all reader if we have made any mistakes through this book. We deliberately understand that this book need improvement. We really consider your feedback to get this book better.

Sincerely,

Taufik Hidayat

(Coordinator Project)

THE CONTRIBUTORS

This book was collaboratively composed by LibreOffice Indonesia community through Internet as medium. The contributors was introduced below.

Cover Designer

Ade Malsasa Akbar <teknoloid@gmail.com>

Language Editors

1. Ahmad Romadhon Hidayatullah <reaamina@gmail.com> (Chapter 1 dan Chapter 4)
2. Ade Malsasa Akbar <teknoloid@gmail.com> (Chapter 1 dan Chapter 2)
3. Nugroho <nugroho.redbuff@gmail.com> (Chapter 21)
4. Faiq Aminuddin <dampuawang@gmail.com> (Chapter 1 s/d Chapter 29)
5. Taufik Hidayat <yumtaufik1997@gmail.com> (Chapter 4 dan Chapter 7)
6. Andhika Prasetyo <chupunk3@gmail.com> (Chapter 5)

Book Editors

1. Taufik Hidayat <yumtaufik1997@gmail.com>
2. Nur Kholis <khokunsmile@gmail.com>
3. Abdul Aziz <ingejosmu1048576@gmail.com>

The Writers

1. Ade Malsasa Akbar <teknoloid@gmail.com> (Chapter 1, Chapter 2, Chapter 6, Chapter 7 dan Chapter 18)

2. Muhammad Yuga Nugraha <myugan59@gmail.com> (Chapter 3)

3. Mochammad Nur Afandi <muh.afandi.fandi@gmail.com> (Chapter 8)

4. Mukafi <kakafi30@gmail.com> (Chapter 4 dan Chapter 9)

5. Taufik Hidayat <yumtaufik1997@gmail.com> (Chapter 5, Chapter 10, Chapter 12, Chapter 13, Chapter 14 dan Chapter 17)

6. Anto Samalona <ansamsoftdev@gmail.com> (Chapter 11)

7. Sasongko Bawono <sasongko262@gmail.com> (Chapter 15 dan Chapter 16)

8. Nur Kholis <khokunsmile@gmail.com> (Chapter 19, Chapter 25 dan Chapter 27)

9. Azis Rahmat Pratama <azis.pratama@gmail.com> (Chapter 20)

10. Azid <paindustry@yahoo.com> (Chapter 21)

11. Sukamto <kamtono@gmail.com> (Chapter 22)

12. Buono <kangbuono@gmail.com> (Chapter 23 dan Chapter 26)

13. Rahmat Kafabih (Kafabih/KR) <kafalterbang@gmail.com> (Chapter 24)

14. Muhammad Irwan Andriawan <andriawan2014@gmail.com> (Chapter 28)

15. Taufik Mulyana <nothinux@nothinux.id> (Chapter 29)

The Translators

1. <ari> (Chapter 26)
2. Thoriq Kemal <thoriqcemal@gmail.com> (Chapter 12, Chapter 13, Chapter 25)

3. Astrida Atni Ayu Mahardini <astriddini7@gmail.com> (Chapter 5, Chapter 17, Chapter 18, Chapter 19, Chapter 22)

4. Azis R. Pratama <azis.pratama@gmail.com> (Chapter 20, Chapter 23

5. Faiq Aminuddin <faiq.aminuddin.demak@gmail.com> (Chapter 15)

6. Ilham Akbar <ilhamsahil05@gmail.com> (Chapter 6, Chapter 7, Chapter 14)

7. kucingsebelah <meongpus@hi2.in> (Chapter 11, Chapter 16)

8. Mochammad Nur Afandi <localanu@gmail.com> (Chapter 8)

9. Muhammad Fathurridlo <mfathurridlo@gmail.com> (Chapter 1, Chapter 3, Chapter 4)

10. Muhammad Irwan Andriawan <andriawan2014@gmail.com> (Preface, The Contributors, Technical Book Preparation, Chapter 24, Chapter 27, Chapter 28, Chapter 29)

11. Raymon Rahmadhani <raymon.rahmadhani@gmail.com> (Chapter 2, Chapter 9, Chapter 10)

12. Risma Fahrul Amin <rismafahrulamin@gmail.com> (Chapter 21)

TECHNICAL BOOK PREPARATION

This part was written as technical guide for all designate writers of this book.

Deadline	30 October 2016
Book scope	LibreOffice Writer
Pages count	220 pages
Font	Liberation Serif
Font size	12 pt
Space	1,5
Alignment	Justified
Format	This Document should be written in .odt format (LibreOffice, OpenOffice, Calligra Office)
LibreOffice Version	4.x s/d 5.x
Minimum Contribution	One chapter per contributor

If you desire to write a chapter, we recommend using standard LibreOffice Writer version 4.x s/d 5.x. You are not confined using any kind of GNU/Linux distros in contributing a chapter.

Heading of chapter should use heading 1, for example chapter 1 Introducing LibreOffice. For sub-chapter, you should use heading 2, for example explaining LibreOffice History. Under sub-chapter, you should enclose Copyright © 2016 <your name> <your email>. **Just write down your experience. Never wait something which does not exist yet. For further explanation, please refer to each existing chapter.**

TABLE OF CONTENTS

"Mari Menggunakan Aplikasi Free and Open Source Software dan Selamatkan Bangsa dari Pembajakan Perangkat Lunak"

(Virgo Tri Septo Anggoro – Anggota BLOI)

CHAPTER 1

INTRODUCTION TO LIBREOFFICE

Copyright © 2016 Ade Malsasa Akbar <teknoloid@gmail.com>

Translated by Muhammad Fathurridlo <mfathurridlo@gmail.com>

LibreOffice

LibreOffice is a free software as office software (office suite) which developed from OpenOffice.org by The Document Foundation organization and available for GNU/Linux, Windows, and Mac.

As an office software, LibreOffice has word processor, spreadsheet, and presentation programs by the name of **Writer**, **Calc**, and **Impress**. The native document format of the three programs is **ODT**, **ODS**, and **ODP** respectively. By default, LibreOffice supports ISO standard document format, that is **OpenDocument Format** (ODF) as a standard (and also supports Microsoft OOXML document formats).

When mentioning about functionality, LibreOffice is equal to Microsoft Office software (which are only available for Windows and Mac). LibreOffice is the most popular office software which becomes built-in program in many GNU/Linux distributions. The official website of The Document Foundation is **https://www.documentfoundation.org** and the official website of LibreOffice is http://libreoffice.org.

The History of LibreOffice

LibreOffice was developed in 2010 based on a free software source code called OpenOffice.org. This is because Oracle (a popular proprietary software company) acquired Sun Microsystem company that maintain OpenOffice.org in early 2010.

The former developers of OpenOffice.org are worried that Oracle will turn the free software into proprietary software, so some of them resign from Oracle project and then create a derivative of OpenOffice.org called LibreOffice. The former developers of OpenOffice.org then formed an organization called The Document Foundation which currently leads LibreOffice software development project.

Years	Events
1985	StarWriter 1.0 was started by Marco Borries (founder of StarDivision company).
1985 and up	StarWriter changed its name to StarOffice.
1999	Sun Microsystem acquired StarDivision company.
2000	Sun announced StarOffice 5.2 software as free software (LGPL). The first http://openoffice.org site appeared.
2001	OpenOffice reached 1 million downloads.
2002	OpenOffice.org 1.0 released.
2010	Oracle acquired Sun Microsystem.
2010	The announcement of The Document Foundation formation.
2011	The Document Foundation released an early version of LibreOffice. LibreOffice has reached 7,5 million downloads in January – October period.

Table 1: LibreOffice's timeline

Here is a picture about LibreOffice's History

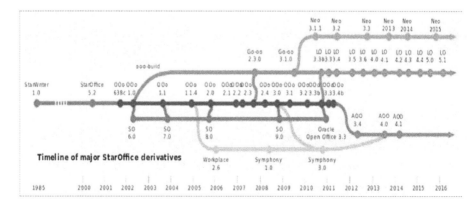

Picture 1: LibreOffice's history

LibreOffice's License

LibreOffice is a free software which licensed under **Mozilla Public License 2.0** as officially stated in https://www.libreoffice.org/about-us/licenses and in every copy of LibreOffice program itself, accessed through **Help > License Information** menu, or inside of LICENSE file.

The third-party software components included in LibreOffice are licensed under the GNU General Public License, the GNU Lesser General Public License, the Apache License, and the CreativeCommons Attribution-ShareAlike. All of LibreOffice's license component can be read in the same place as already mentioned above.

Picture 2: LibreOffice license information

LibreOffice and Microsoft Office Program Comparison

LibreOffice major components are similar with Microsoft Office:

Component	LibreOffice	Microsoft Office
Word Processor	Writer	Word
Spreadsheet	Calc	Excel
Presentation	Impress	PowerPoint

Table 2: The comparison between LibreOffice and Microsoft Office components

LibreOffice Features

- Save and open ODF (Open Document Format) files perfectly.

- Export ODF document into flat XML.

- Import Microsoft Visio and Microsoft Publisher documents.

- Open, edit, and save Microsoft OOXML documents (.docx, .xlsx, .pptx). These document formats are popular on Microsoft Office 2007 until Microsoft Office 2016.

- Open, edit, and save binary-proprietary document format from Microsoft (.doc, .xls, .ppt). These document formats are popular on older Microsoft Office version (before Microsoft Office 2007).

- Save documents as PDF format.

- Add comments and annotations inside the document.

- Remote control application for presentation purpose.

- Use CMIS Protocol for collaboration, newest feature that allows user for collaborating with other user when doing online projects.

Interface

Here are some interfaces of LibreOffice Writer on GNU/Linux operating system:

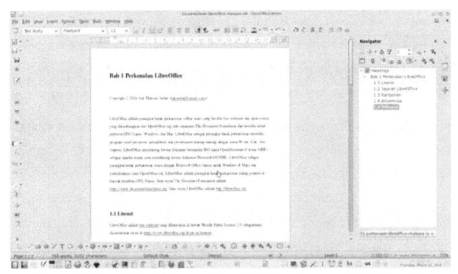

Picture 3: LibreOffice Writer version 4.3.0.4 interface on GNU/Linux Ubuntu

12.04 LTS with KDE 4.10.3 Desktop Environment

Picture 4: LibreOffice Writer version 5.1.1.2 on GNU/Linux Ubuntu

14.04 LTS with Unity 7.2.6 Desktop Environment

LibreOffice Versions

LibreOffice is available in two different major versions, apart from the development versions (numbered release candidates and dated nightly builds). The versions are designed and customized for different user needs. The numbering convention of each release is set with three numbers separated by periods. The **first** number is a large branch number, the **second** number usually signifies minor changes, and the **third** indicates a minor release focusing on bug fixes. LibreOffice specifies two versions of the release as:

- **"Fresh"** – "Fresh" - releases the latest bug fixes from the current big (branch) version, which contains various latest feature additions, but there may be bugs not found in the "Still" release.
- **"Still"** (formerly known as "Stable") – recent bug fixes from previous major versions. which have been through several months of bug fixes and recommended for users who are more concerned with stability than enhancements (feature enhancements). For example, in September 2015, 5.0.2 is a Fresh release, and 4.4.5 is a Still release. When this section is written, LibreOffice latest version is version 5.2, with some improvements, such as:
- Newer user interface.
- Support for writing files to cloud servers (cloud computing)
- Carries support for ODF 1.2 document format standards.
- LibreOffice Calc has significantly improved features.

Picture 5: LibreOffice version 5.1 startup interface (splash screen) on Ubuntu 14.04 LTS

Important References

Here the author convey a number of internet links related to LibreOffice. This link is divided into official links, official documentation links, unofficial documentation links, and some additions.

- LibreOffice official website (the software): http://libreoffice.org
- The Document Foundation official website (organization): http://documentfoundation.org
- LibreOffice at Wikipedia: https://en.wikipedia.org/wiki/LibreOffice
- Official LibreOffice documentation books: http://www.libreoffice.org/get-help/documentation/
- Official LibreOffice documentation books (ultimate version): https://wiki.documentfoundation.org/Documentation/Publications
- LibreOffice source code (website): https://www.libreoffice.org/about-us/source-code/
- LibreOffice source code (Git server): https://cgit.freedesktop.org/libreoffice
- Paid technical LibreOffice support (professional): https://www.libreoffice.org/get-help/professional-support/
- Official LibreOffice mailing list: https://www.libreoffice.org/get-help/mailing-lists/

- Contributing to LibreOffice guides: https://www.libreoffice.org/community/get-involved/
- Donate to LibreOffice project: https://www.libreoffice.org/donate/

User Guides from The Community

- **The Frugal Computer Guy** http://thefrugalcomputerguy.com provides so many videos about LibreOffice tutorials.
- **GoFree** http://www.gofree.com provides written guidance about LibreOffice.
- **Tutorials for OpenOffice** http://www.tutorialsforopenoffice.org provides written guidance about OpenOffice.org.
  Note: LibreOffice is developed from OpenOffice.org source code.

CHAPTER 2

INTRODUCTION TO OPENDOCUMENT FORMAT

Translated by Raymon Rahmadhani <raymon.rahmadhani@gmail.com>

LibreOffice embraces the standard digital documentation format called OpenDocument Format (ODF) which is published by OASIS organization. The ODF standard itself had been standardized by ISO (International Standardization Organization) as an International office suite document standard. The ODF standard has three main formats, that are **.odt** (word processor), **.ods** (spreadsheet), and **.odp** (presentation). All of them are manifested into three LibreOffice programs; **Writer**, **Calc**, and **Impress**.

Introduction

The consideration of software, hardware, and standard are commonly acknowledge in the world of computer science. So does in developing an office suite application which is not built without any consideration at all, but it should embrace a certain document standard. In term of this book, the writer compared between two platforms, which are Microsoft Office and LibreOffice. Therefore, as a software, both of them are compared as Microsoft Office and LibreOffice. Meanwhile, as a standard, both are compared as OOXML and ODF. For those who plan to *migrate* to LibreOffice platform seriously should understand the following considerations. Here is the table that shows a brief explanation of both standard.

Platform Microsoft		Platform LibreOffice	
Standard name	Microsoft OOXML	Standard name	OpenDocument Format
Publisher	Microsoft	Publisher	OASIS
Software name	Microsoft Office	Software name	LibreOffice
Software Developer	Microsoft	Software Developer	The Document Foundation
Publication of specification	http://www.ecma-international.org/publications/standards/Ecma-376.htm	Publication of specification	https://www.oasis-open.org/committees/office
Standard number	ISO/IEC 29500	Standard number	ISO/IEC 26300
ISO approval	http://www.iso.org/iso/home/store/catalogue_tc/catalogue_detail.htm? csnumber=61750	ISO approval	http://www.iso.org/iso/home/store/catalogue_tc/catalogue_detail.htm? csnumber=43485

Table 3: Standard comparison between Microsoft and LibreOffice Platform

The Table of ODF and Its Programs

Format	Program	Function
.odt	LibreOffice Writer	Word processor
.ods	LibreOffice Calc	Number processor
.odp	LibreOffice Impress	Presentation processor
.odg	LibreOffice Drawing	Picture processor

Table 4: The Table of ODF and Its Programs

Comparison between ODF and Microsoft Format

In this case, the term "Standard" is a standard which is created by OASIS and Microsoft in the other hand. Microsoft has two kinds of standard format, they are **closed** document format (.doc, etc.) and OOXML document format (.docx, etc.). Meanwhile, OASIS has 1 standard format only, that is **ODF**. This section is trying to show the difference between Microsoft and OASIS standard format. Furthermore, it also compares between programs which embrace Microsoft standard and OASIS standard.

Table of Closed Format versus ODF:

Microsoft's Closed Formats	ODF Format
.doc	.odt
.xls	.ods
.ppt	.odp

Table 5: Closed Format and ODF Comparison

The Table of OOXML versus ODF Format:

OOXML Format	ODF Format
.docx	.odt
.xlsx	.ods
.pptx	.odp

Table 6: OOXML and ODF Format Comparison

The Table of the OOXML based programs versus ODF based programs:

OOXML based programs	ODF based programs
Microsoft Word	LibreOffice Writer
Microsoft Excel	LibreOffice Calc
Microsoft PowerPoint	LibreOffice Impress

Table 7: OOXML and ODF Based Programs Comparison

The Table of the Alternative ODF Based Programs

The following table presents the information about softwares which support OpenDocument format as an alternative to LibreOffice. Furthermore, it presents free software only wthout inclusion of proprietary software.

Format	Function	LibreOffice	LibreOffice Alternative
.odt	Word Processor	Writer	OpenOffice Writer, Calligra Words, Abiword
.ods	Number Processor	Calc	OpenOffice Calc, Calligra Sheets, Gnumeric
.odp	Presentation Processor	Impress	OpenOffice Impress, Calligra Stage

Table 8: LibreOffice's Alternative with ODF Based Programs

The Table of Free Office Suite Program as a LibreOffice Alternative

The following table presents the office suite programs, which are licensed as free software, as the LibreOffice alternative. Moreover, all of the following programs support OpenDocument format.

Name	License	Descriptions
Apache OpenOffice	Apache License 2.0	• Provides word processor, spreadsheet, and presentation; • Developed by Sun OpenOffice.org, Sun StarOffice. • LibreOffice starts up development. • Available in all GNU/Linux distribution. • Actively Developed.
Calligra Suite	GNU GPL, GNU LGPL	• Provides *word processor*, *spreadsheet*, and *presentation*; • Developed by Koffice;

		• Available in all GNU/Linux distribution. • Actively Developed.
KOffice	GNU GPL, GNU LGPL	• *Provides word processor, spreadsheet, and presentation;* • Additional features. • Has been terminated.
NeoOffice	GNU GPL	• *Provides word processor, spreadsheet, and presentation;* • Developed by Sun OpenOffice.org. • Built especially for Apple OS X. • Actively Developed.

Table 9: Free Office Suite Program as a LibreOffice Alternative

The Table of Proprietary Softwares which Support ODF

Program's Name	Description
Microsoft Office	Supports ODF since 2010 to 2016 version.
Google Docs	Supports ODF partially.
SoftMaker Office	Supports ODF partially.
IBM Lotus Symphony	Supports ODF.
Corel WordPerfect Office	Supports ODF since X4 versions.

Table 10: Proprietary Softwares which Support ODF

Reference:

https://en.wikipedia.org/wiki/OpenDocument

https://en.wikipedia.org/wiki/Comparison_of_Office_Open_XML_and_OpenDocument

https://linuxdreambox.wordpress.com/2016/01/10/support-open-document-format/

CHAPTER 3

INTRODUCTION TO LIBREOFFICE WRITER INTERFACE

Copyright © 2016 Muhammad Yuga Nugraha <myugan59@gmail.com>

Translated by Muhammad Fathurridlo <mfathurridlo@gmail.com>

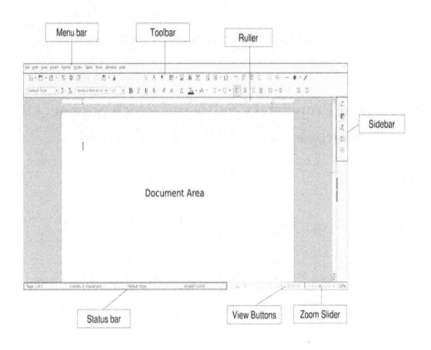

Picture 6: LibreOffice Writer interface

Picture description:

Interface	Description
Menu Bar	Runs LibreOffice Writer commands

Toolbar	Buttons that can be used to run LibreOffice commands.
Ruler	Ruler for knowing real document size.
Side Bar	Shows buttons from Properties, Styles and Formatting, Gallery, and Navigator.
Document Area	Work space
Status Bar	Shows current document informations such as total page, total words, and total characters.
View Buttons	Changes document view model.
Zoom Slider	Works as Zoom In and Zoom Out button (enlarging or shrinking document view).

Table 11: Picture information about LibreOffice Writer interface

CHAPTER 4

INTRODUCTION TO LIBREOFFICE

WRITER SIDEBAR

Translated by Muhammad Fathurridlo <mfathurridlo@gmail.com>

Sidebar is a dock that located on the right of document area. Sidebar contains tool properties, styles and formatting, gallery and navigator. **To enable** sidebar, click on View Menu, and then choose Sidebar. The features of Sidebar are shown on the pictures below.

Sidebar

Picture 7: Sidebar position on LibreOffice Writer

Sidebar has four features, there are: Properties, Character, Paragraph and Page.

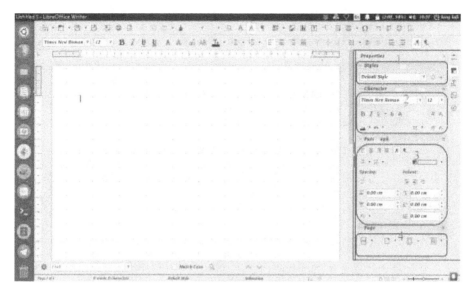

Picture 8: Sidebar features

Properties

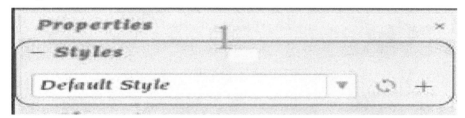

Picture 9: Properties Features

Description:

Styles: Change the style of writing. For example, we will write the phrase "INTRODUCTION TO LIBREOFFICE" and want to be a chapter title, then highlight the "title" option in the Style option. Then the text will be the title with the centering format and bold without additional effort pressing the Ctrl + E combination and Ctrl + B on the keyboard.

Character

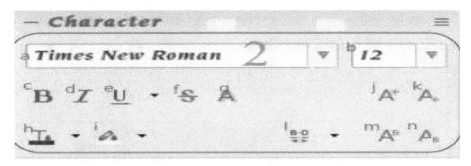

Picture 10: Character features

Descriptions:

a.	*Font Type*	To change the font type
b.	*Font size*	To change the font size
c.	*Bold*	To change the typing to thick-typing
d.	*Italic*	To change the typing to tilt-typing
e.	*Underline*	To convert the text to underlined text
f.	*Strikethrough*	To give a strike into the text
g.	*Shadows*	To give a shadow on a text
h.	*Font color*	To change the color on a text
i..	*Highlight color*	To give background color on a text
j.	*Increase font size*	To increase the font size
k.	*Decrease font size*	To decrease the font size
l.	*Character spacing*	To change the space between characters
m.	*Superscript*	To change the characters into slightly above of the normal text line.
n.	*Subscript*	To change the characters into slightly below of the normal text line.

Paragraph

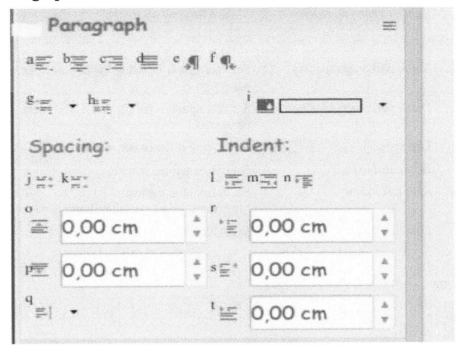

Picture 11: Paragraph features

Descriptions:

a.	*Align left*	Set the typing to be flat on the left side
b.	*Center horizontally*	Set the typing to be flat on the center side
c.	*Align right*	Set the typing to be flat on the right side
d.	*Justified*	Set the typing to be flat on the right and left side.
e.	*Left to Right*	Start typing from left to right direction.
f.	*Right to Left*	Start typing from to right to left direction.
g.	*Bullet*	Create a symbolic list
h.	*Numbering*	Create an alphabetic or numeric list
i.	*Background color*	Give color to the background
j.	*Increase paragraph spacing*	Increase paragraph spacing
k.	*Decrease paragraph spacing*	Decrease paragraph spacing
l.	*Increase indent*	Increase the left indent of the current paragraph so the text will indented inside
m.	*Decrease indent*	Restore / decrease the left indent of the

current paragraph

n.	*Switch to hanging indent*	Make a hanging paragraph
o.	*Above paragraph spacing*	Set paragraph spacing with previous paragraph
p.	*Below paragraph spacing*	Set paragraph spacing with the next paragraph
q.	*Line spacing*	Set spacing distance between lines
r.	*Before text indent*	Set indent before the text
s.	*After text indent*	Set indent after the text Mengatur tabulasi setelah tulisan
t.	*First line indent*	Set indent only the first line

Page

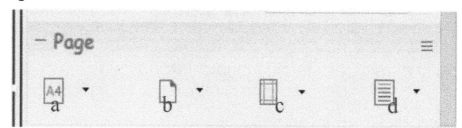

Picture 12: Page features

Descriptions:

a.	*Size*	Set the document paper size
b.	*Orientation*	Set the document orientation (potrait or landscape)
c.	*Margin*	Set the document margin
d.	*Columns*	Set the document column

CHAPTER 5

GETTING ACQUAINTED WITH THE MENU BAR IN LIBREOFFICE WRITER

Translated by Astrida Atni Ayu Mahardini <astriddini7@gmail.com>

Out of sight, out of mind, this phrase actually is a reality. If we don't be familiar with something, then it is impossible for us to love or having interest with it. Because everything has to go through the stages of getting to know in advance, we can be next new familiar and loved it/favored him. Likewise with LibreOffice, impossible to use it continuously if we don't ' get acquainted ' first with him.

In this chapter, the author will discuss the sub-Sub menus on the Menu Bar in LibreOffice Writer. Each Sub Menu on LibreOffice Writer is a unity that cannot be separated and intertwined each other. The author uses LibreOffice Writer 4.2.8.2 version with operating system OS Grombyang (GrOS).

Please note that the author uses LibreOffice Writer consists of 9 Menu: File, Edit, View, Insert, Format, Table, Tools, Window, and Help. In this chapter, the author frequently used the word "Menu", "Sub Menu" and "Sub-Sub Menu". It is located on the Menu Bar menu, Sub Menu is the Menu that is present on the Menu and Sub Menu is the Menu that is present on the Sub Menu.

The File Menu

The file menu has functionality to open, close, save, print, export and preview the document. Below is a picture and description of the Sub Menu on the File menu. Sub Menu File: New, Open, Recent Documents, Wizards, Templates, Close, Save, Save As, Save As, Save Copy All, Reload, Versions, Export, Export a PDF, Send Us,

Properties, Digital Signatures, Preview in a Web Browser, the Page Preview, Print, Printer Settings and Exit LibreOffice.

Picture 13: The Menu File

Descriptions:

1.	*New*	Start a new document.
2.	*Open*	Create document that are never stored.
3.	*Recent Documents*	Create document that never opened before.
4.	*Wizards*	Display the wizard.
5.	*Templates*	Create template document on LibreOffice Writer.
6.	*Close*	Close the active document.
7.	*Save*	Save the active document.
8.	*Save As*	Save the active document with a name and format or a different location.
9.	*Save As Copy*	Save and copy document.
10.	*Save All*	Save all document.
11.	*Reload*	Refresh/refresh the document.

12.	*Versions*	Save the document with read-only format.
13.	*Export*	Export the document with different formatting.
14.	*Export As Pdf*	Exporting a PDF formatted documents.
15.	*Send*	Send the document to other media such as e-mail.
16.	*Properties*	View and manage the information document.
17.	*Digital Signatures*	Add a digital signature.
18.	*Preview In Web Browser*	Preview the document in the web browser.
19.	*Page Preview*	Preview the document before printing.
20.	*Print*	To print the document.
21.	*Printer Settings*	Set the tool print (Printer).
22.	*Exit LibreOffice*	Out of LibreOffice.

Each Sub Menu in the File menu, has a Sub Sub Menu or options respectively. The following is a function of the options/Sub-Sub menus on the Sub Menu in the File Menu.

Sub-Sub Menu New

Sub's menu new is used to start a new document. Suppose you want to create a new document, you can select Sub Menu New as an option. New sub menus have a Sub-Sub menus like: Text Document (LibreOffice Writer), Spreadsheet (LibreOffice Calc), Presentation (LibreOffice Impress), Drawing (LibreOffice Draw), Database (LibreOffice Base), HTML Document (LibreOffice Writer/Web), an XML Form Document (XML Document Form LibreOffice), Master Document (LibreOffice Writer), Formula (LibreOffice Math), Labels (LibreOffice Writer), Business Card (LibreOffice Writer) and Templates.

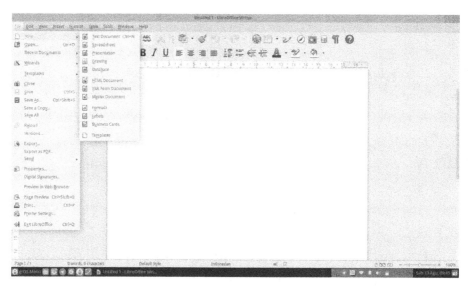

Picture 14: Sub-Sub Menu New

Descriptions:

1. *Text Document*   Create documents with LibreOffice Writer
2. *Spreadsheet*   Create a document/workbook with LibreOffice Calc
3. *Presentation*   Create presentations with LibreOffice Impress
4. *Drawing*   Create documents with LibreOffice Draw
5. *Database*   Create a database with LibreOffice Base
6. *HTML Document*   Create HTML documents with LibreOffice Writer/Web
7. *XML   Form* Create an XML document with an XML Document
    Document   Form LibreOffice
8. *Master Document*   Create and manage documents, example a book with
    many chapters with LibreOffice Writer
9. *Formula*   Create mathematical formulas with LibreOffice Math
10. *Labels*   Create labels with LibreOffice Writer
11. *Bussiness Cards*   Make business cards with LibreOffice Writer
12. *Templates*   Create a document template with LibreOffice Writer

Sub-Sub Menu Recent Documents

Sub's menu recent document serves to open documents that never opened or created before. The Sub Menu functions can be as a shortcut to open the documents that have been made before.

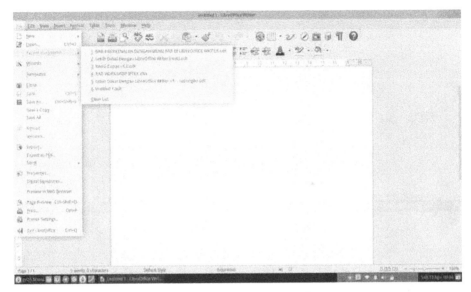

Picture 15: Sub-Sub Menu Recent Documents

Sub-Sub Menu Wizards

Sub's menu wizards has functionality to display wizards. This Sub Menu is used to create a document in the format you want in available the template. Suppose you want to create a letter, you can select the option Letter as template. You can try a wide kind of templates provided by LibreOffice Writer to create documents according to your needs.

Sub's Menu on Wizards: Letter, Fax, Agenda, Presentation, Web Page, Document Converter, Euro Converter and the Address of the Data Source.

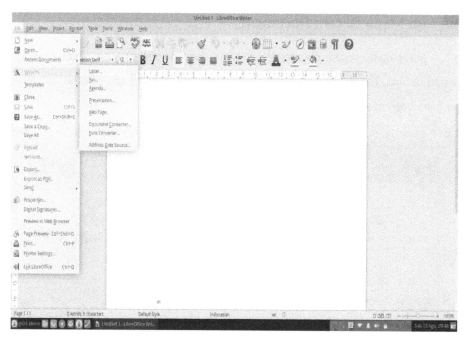

Picture 16: Sub-Sub Menu Wizards

Descriptions:

1. *Letter*   Create a letter with the specified template

2. *Fax*   Create a fax document with the specified template

3. *Agenda*   Create an agenda with the specified template

4. *Presentation*   Create presentations with the specified template

5. *Web Page*   Publish the document to the cloud with a specified template

6. *Document Converter*   Convert the document to other formats form

7. *Euro Converter*   Convert the document to format currencies other European countries

8. *Address Data Source*   Insert the address of the data source into a document

Sub-Sub Menu Templates

Sub's menu templates serves to create a document template on LibreOffice Writer. For example, you want to make a CV (Curriculum Vitae) to apply for a job.

With the template provided by the LibreOffice Writer, you do not need to create and design your own CV. This will greatly facilitate the beginner to create their own CV. You can also set/change Your template by converting the format on the options Filter.

Sub's Menu Templates: Save As Templates and Manage.

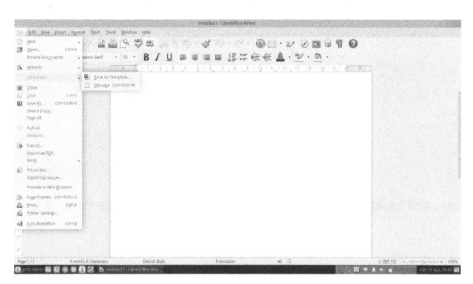

Picture 17: Sub-Sub Menu Templates

Descriptions:

1. *Save As Templates*   Save the document as a template

2. *Manage*   Create a document with a template that has been provided

Sub-Sub Menu Send

Sub's menu send has functionality to send the document to other media. Suppose you want to send a document via e-mail or bluetooth. In addition, if you want to create an abstract or paper for scientific paper, you can take advantage of the features of AutoAbstract.

Sub's Menu-Send consists of an E-mail, the Document is the E-mail as Text Document, Email us the E-mail as Microsoft Word, PDF, Send Via Bluetooth, Create a Master Document, Create an HTML Document, Outline to Presentation, Outline to the Clipboard, Create AutoAbstract and AutoAbstract to Presentation.

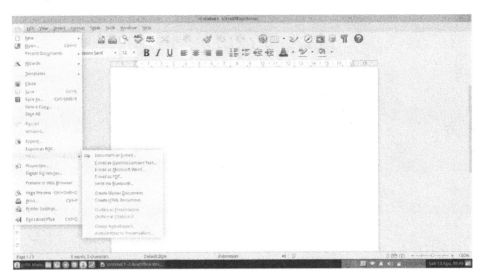

Picture 18: Sub-Sub Menu Send

Descriptions:

1.	*Document as E-mail*	Send documents as electronic mail
2.	*E-mail as Document Text*	Send the document through electronic mail as the document shaped ODT
3.	*Email as Microsoft Word*	Send the document through electronic mail in Microsoft Word format
4.	*E-mail as PDF*	Send the document through electronic mail as PDF
5.	*Send Via Bluetooth*	Send documents via Bluetooth
6.	*Create Master Document*	Create a Master Document
7.	*Create HTML Document*	Create a document in HTML form
8.	*Outline to Presentation*	Create a document presentation form
9.	*Outline to Clipboard*	Make the document shaped the Clipboard
10.	*Create AutoAbstract*	Make abstract
11.	*AutoAbstract to Presentation*	Make the abstract to the form of presentation

The Menu Edit

The menu edit is used to edit, copy, paste, find, replace, find and replace, insert a table of contents and bibliography, linking, selecting and comparing documents.

Sub's the edit menu: Undo, Redo, Repeat, Cut, Copy, Paste, Pate Special, Select Text, Selection Mode, Select All, Changes, Compare Document, Find, Find and Replace, AutoText, Exchange Database, the Fields, the Footnote/Endnote, Bibliography Entry, Index Entry, hyperlinks, Links, Plug-ins, ImageMap and Object.

Picture 19: The Edit Menu

Descriptions:

1.	*Undo*	Undo or step (back to previous command)
2.	*Redo*	Repeat orders or canceled step (towards the Undo command)
3.	*Repeat*	Repeat user command
4.	*Cut*	Cut a piece of writing or object
5.	*Copy*	Copy writing or objects.
6.	*Paste*	Attach the post or object that has been copied
7.	*Paste Special*	Display the results of a copy with additional commands

8.	*Select Text*	Select writings
9.	*Selection Mode*	Set the mode selection
10.	*Select All*	Select the entire writing
11.	*Changes*	Set the document changes
12.	*Compare Document*	Compare documents
13.	*Find*	Find writings
14.	*Find & Replace*	Find and replace writing
15.	*AutoText*	Make writing automatically
16.	*Exchange Database*	Set Exchange database
17.	*Fields*	*Set field*
18.	*Footnote/Endnote*	Provide footnotes or endnotes
19.	*Index Entry*	*Set the index entry*
20.	*Bibliography Entry*	Set Bibliography Entry
21.	*Hyperlink*	Set *hyperlink*
22.	*Links*	Set up/form links (relationships)
23.	*Plug-in*	Set the plug-in
24.	*ImageMap*	View/manage image maps
25.	*Object*	Set the object that has been inserted

Each Sub Menu in the Edit Menu, and has Sub Sub Menu or options respectively. The following is a function of the options/Sub-Sub menus on the Sub Menu in the File Menu.

Sub-Sub Menu Selection Mode

Sub's menu selection mode serves to set the mode selection. For example, you want to change a sentence with another sentence. You can use the feature Selection Mode to select the sentence, and then replace them as you want.

Sub's menu selection mode is Standard and Block Area.

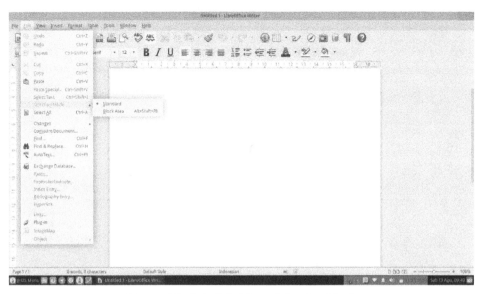

Picture 20: Sub-Sub Menu Selection Mode

Descriptions:

1. *Selection Mode*   Select the writing mode selection
2. *Block Area*   Choose a writing block area

Sub-Sub Menu Changes

Sub's menu changes serve to set up change document. For example, if you want to comment on a text, you can use the option Comment.

Sub's Menu Changes is: Record, Protect Records, Show, Accept or Reject, Comment, Next Change and Previous Change, Merge Document.

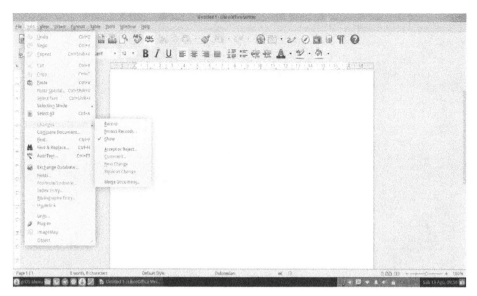

Picture 21: Sub-Sub Menu Changes

Descriptions:

1. *Record* — Record changes
2. *Protect Records* — Protect recordings by giving your password
3. *Show* — Publish your changes
4. *Accept or Reject* — Accept or cancel a recording
5. *Comment* — Provide comments on the document
6. *Next Change* — See further changes
7. *Previous Change* — See previous changes
8. *Merge Document* — Merge document before and after the edit by more than one person

The View Menu

The view menu is used to display the text boundaries, toolbars, pictures, status bar, rulers, scrollbars, etc. on the document. Sub Menu View: Print Layout, Web Layout, Toolbars, Status bars, Input Method Status, Ruler, Text Boundaries, Field Shadings, Field Names, Non-printing Characters, Hidden Paragraphs, Comments, Data Sources, Navigator, Sidebar, Full Screen and Zoom.

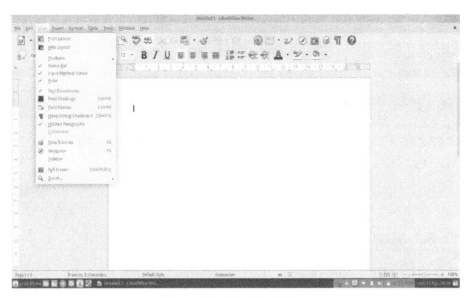

Picture 22: The View Menu

Descriptions:

1.	*Print Layout*	Display the print layout
2.	*Web Layout*	Display our document editing when it appears in a web browser
3.	*Toolbars*	Show or hides the toolbar's
4.	*Status Bar*	Show or hides the status document
5.	*Input Method Status*	Track the status of the input method
6.	*Ruler*	Show or hide the rulers above and to the left of the work area
7.	*Text Boundaries*	Show or hides margin limits in the work area
8.	*Field Shadings*	Show or hide the shadow field
9.	*Field Names*	Show/hide a field name
10.	*Nonprinting Characters*	Show or hides the characters are not printed
11.	*Hidden Paragraphs*	Enable or disable hidden paragraph
12.	*Comments*	Make a comment
13.	*Data Sources*	Display or hide the data source
14.	*Navigator*	Show or hide the menu Navigator
15.	*Sidebar*	Display the toolbar menu Sidebar at the side of the

		documents/work area
16.	*Full Screen*	Create a full-screen mode
17.	*Zoom*	Set the magnification of a document display

Each Sub Menu in the View Menu, has a Sub Sub Menu or options respectively. The following is a function of the options/Sub-Sub menus on the Sub Menu in the View Menu.

Sub-Sub Menu Toolbars

Sub's menu toolbars used to insert text objects, fontwork, table, picture, frame, media playback and so on. The toolbar can be said as a shortcut that aims to make it easy for users in the work. So, the users who work with using LibreOffice Writer can work in comfort.

Sub's Menu Toolbars is 3D Settings, Align Objects, Bullets and Numbering, Changes, Drawing, Drawing Object Properties, Find, Fontwork, Form, Form Design, Control the Form Navigation, Formating, Frame, Insert, Media Playback, Navigation, OLE-Object, Picture, Standard, Standard (Viewing Mode), Table, Text objects, Tools, Customize formulas, and Reset.

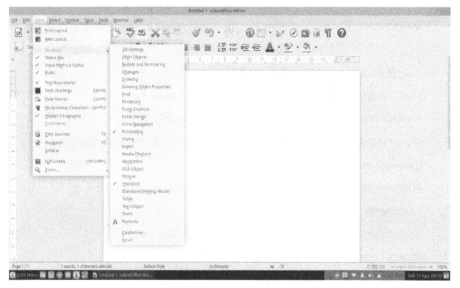

Picture 23: Sub-Sub Menu Toolbars

Descriptions:

1. *3D Settings* — 3D Settings toolbar
2. *Align Objects* — Setting the direction of the object toolbar
3. *Bullets and Numbering* — Bullet and numbering Settings toolbar
4. *Changes* — Toolbar settings change documents
5. *Drawing* — Drawing toolbar
6. *Drawing Object Properties* — Toolbar settings
7. *Find* — Toolbar search writings
8. *Fontwork* — Graphic writing toolbar
9. *Form Controls* — Forms toolbar controls/settings
10. *Form Design* — Form Design toolbar
11. *Form Navigation* — Forms toolbar Navigation
12. *Formatting* — Toolbar to edit the document
13. *Frame* — Insert a picture into a worksheet
14. *Insert* — insert mode toolbar into the toolbar
15. *Media Playback* — Media player toolbar
16. *Navigation* — Sidebar navigation toolbar
17. *OLE-Object* — Toolbar settings object as a link or embedded object
18. *Picture* — Toolbar settings picture
19. *Standard* — Normal mode is the standard toolbar
20. *Standard (Viewing Mode)* — The standard toolbar mode view
21. *Table* — Toolbar settings table
22. *Text Object* — Toolbar text objects
23. *Formula* — Toolbar to insert mathematical formulas
24. *Tools* — Toolbar to insert tool's needed
25. *Customize* — Customize icons on the toolbar
26. *Reset* — Return the entire toolbar settings to its original form

Sub-Sub Menu Zoom

Sub's menu zoom is used to set the display size of the document. Suppose you want to enlarge the screen display of your documents. You can choose the Zoom Sub Menu option and choose the desired display magnification.

Sub's menu zoom is Entire Page, Page Width, Optimal view, 50%, 75%, 100%, 150%, 200% and Zoom.

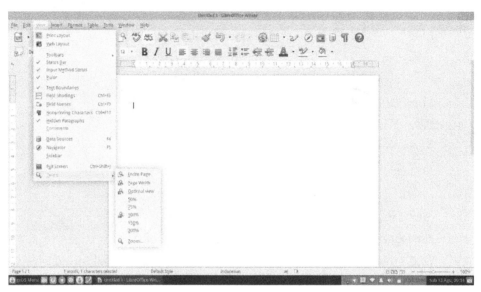

Picture 24: Sub-Sub Menu Zoom

Descriptions:

1.	*Entire Page*	See entire page worksheets in one screen
2.	*Page Width*	Look at the size of the worksheet pages as wide screen
3.	*Optimal view*	See page worksheets are ideally set
4.	*50%*	See the pages worksheet with 50% zoom
5.	*75%*	See worksheet page with magnification of 75%
6.	*100%*	See worksheet page with magnification 100%
7.	*150%*	See page worksheets with 150% zoom
8.	*200%*	See the pages worksheet with 200% magnification
9.	*Zoom*	See worksheet page with zoom mode

The Insert Menu

The Insert menu use to insert an image, header, footnote and endnote, feet, objects, diagrams, special characters, hyperlinks, tables, scripts, caption, bookmarks and etc.

Sub Menu Insert is: Manual Break, Fields, Special Character, Formating Mark, Section, Hyperlink, Header, Footer, Footnote/Endnote, Caption, Bookmark, Cross-reference, Comment, Script, Indexes and Tables, Envelope, Frame, Table, Image, Movie and Sound, Object, Floating Frame and File.

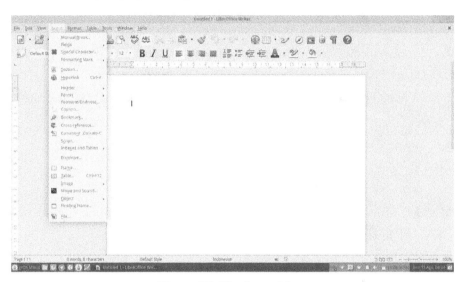

Picture 25: The Insert Menu

Description:

1.	*Manual Break*	Provide a manual break at work page
2.	*Fields*	Insert data that is changed in the document sheets
3.	*Special Character*	Insert special characters
4.	*Formatting Mark*	Paste formatting mark into a worksheet
5.	*Section*	Add section
6.	*Hyperlink*	Providing hyperlinks
7.	*Header*	Provide a heading on a worksheet
8.	*Footer*	Give Away on a worksheet
9.	*Footnote/Endnote*	Provide footnotes and endnotes

10.	*Caption*	Provide a caption on a worksheet
11.	*Bookmark*	Marking an important part
12.	*Cross-reference*	Provide cross-reference
13.	*Comment*	Provide comments on a worksheet
14.	*Script*	Give the script on a worksheet
15.	*Indexes and Tables*	Provides index and tables
16.	*Envelope*	Add envelope
17.	*Frame*	Make layouts one or more columns of text and objects
18.	*Table*	Insert a table into a worksheet
19.	*Image*	Insert a picture into a worksheet
20.	*Movie and Sound*	Providing sound and image
21.	*Object*	Insert object into the worksheet
22.	*Floating Frame*	Insert a floating frame (used in HTML documents-shaped) to display the contents of another file
23.	*File*	Insert a file into a worksheet

Each Sub Menu in the Insert Menu, has a Sub Sub Menu or options respectively. The following is a function of the options/Sub-Sub Sub Menu in the Menu on the Insert Menu.

Sub-Sub Menu Fields

Sub's menu fields used to insert data that is changed, for example is a page number, date and so on. For example, if you enter the page numbering manually then you should edit it multiple times and this will cause not efficiency time. You can use this option to efficiency the time.

Sub's menu fields is: Date, Time, Page Number, Page Count, Subject, Title, Author and Other.

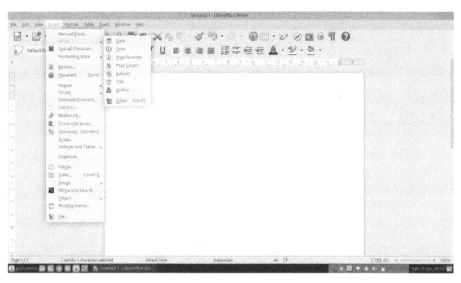

Picture 26: Sub-Sub Menu Fields

Descriptions:

1. *Date*   Provides information on a worksheet

2. *Time*   Provide a description of a time on a worksheet

3. *Page Number*   Give the page numbers on a worksheet

4. *Page Count*   Inserts a large number of pages on a worksheet

5. *Subject*   Inserts a subject on a worksheet

6. *Title*   Provide a title on a worksheet

7. *Author*   Insert description document on a worksheet maker

8. *Other*   Insert another document as a field

Sub-Sub Menu Formatting Mark

This Sub menu is used to set mark formatting using hyphen space or hyphen. Suppose you write and you want to separate the two words, you can use the separator distance with a space or hyphen (-).

Sub's menu formatting mark is: Non-breaking space, Non-breaking hyphen and Optional hyphen.

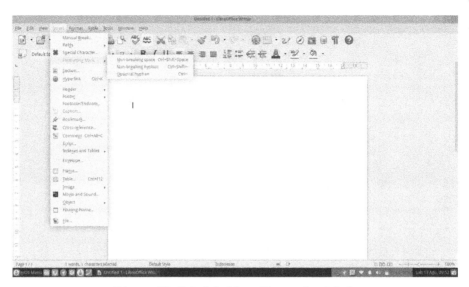

Picture 27: Sub-Sub Menu Formatting Mark

Descriptions:

1. *Non-breaking Space*   Two or more words separated by spaces
2. *Non-breaking Hyphen* Separate two or more words with a dash
3. *Optional Hyphen*   Separate two or more words fit the desired options

Sub-Sub Menu Header

Sub's header menu is used to make header/head. Suppose you want to create a header/head on your document, then you can choose to make the header header/head on your document. If you use a heading in your document, then the header will be automatically active on your next document sheet page.

Sub menu header is Default Style.

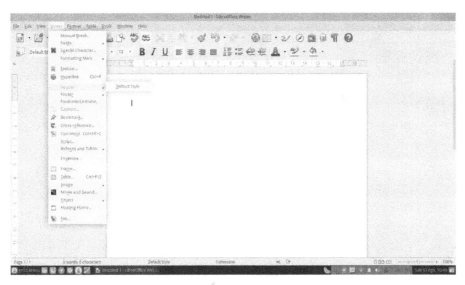

Picture 28: Sub-Sub Menu Header

Descriptions:

Default Style   Choose header/default-style header/default

Sub-Sub Menu Footer

Sub's footer menu is used to make the footer/feet. For example, you want to make a note at the bottom of each page of your document, you can then enable the footer. If you use the footer on your document, then the entry will be automatically active on your next document sheet page.

Sub menu footer is default style.

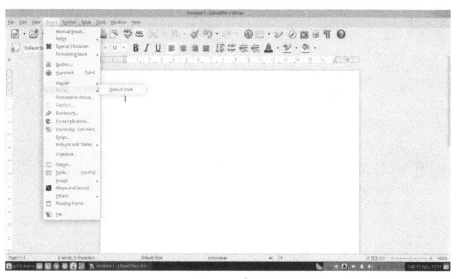

Picture 29: Sub-Sub Menu Footer

Descriptions:

Default Style   Choose footer default style/feet/default

Sub-Sub Menu Indexes and Tables

Sub's menu indexes and tables used to include references and tables and indexes. Suppose you want to create a bibliography, you do not need to create your own format. LibreOffice has been providing its format to facilitate your work.

Sub's menu on indexes and tables is: Entry, Indexes and Tables and Bibliography Entry.

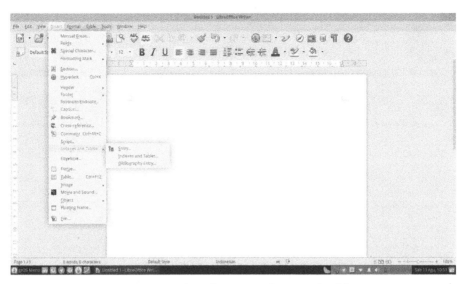

Picture 30: Sub-Sub Menu Indexes and Tables

Descriptions:

1. *Entry*   Inserts index entries
2. *Indexes and Tables*   Insert index and table
3. *Bibliography Entry*   Insert bibliography

Sub-Sub Menu Image

Sub's menu image used to insert images into a worksheet. Suppose you want to insert a picture into your document, you can easily paste it because LibreOffice Writer has prepared for you.

Sub's menu image is: From File, Scan and Fontwork Gallery.

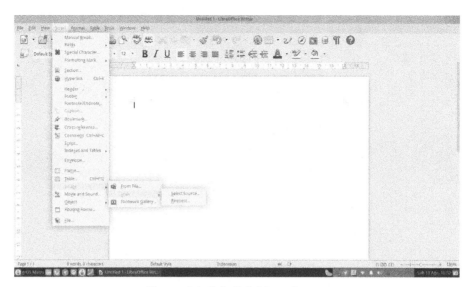

Picture 31: Sub-Sub Menu Image

Descriptions:

1. *From File*   Insert a picture from a file that has been provided previously
2. *Scan*   Insert a picture from a scanned
3. *Fontwork Gallery*   Insert an image via the Gallery fontwork

Sub-Sub Menu Object

Sub's menu object is used to insert object into the worksheet. For example, you want to make the diagram and insert it into your document. You can use the Chart option in the Sub Menu Object.

Sub's Menu Object is: OLE-Object,Plug-In, Formula and Chart.

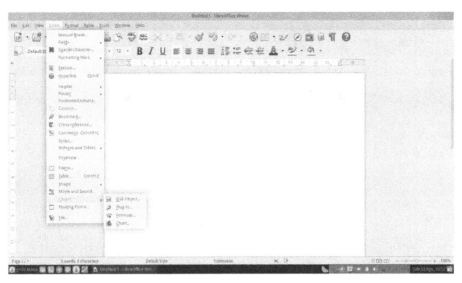

Picture 32: Sub-Sub Menu Object

Descriptions:

1. *OLE-Object*   Paste the object as a link or an object
2. *Plug-In*   Insert plug-in
3. *Formula*   Insert a mathematical formula into a document
4. *Chart*   Insert a chart into a document

The Menu Format

The menu format function to set up the worksheet page, paragraph, insert a bullet and numbering, enable keyboard guide Phonetic Asia, insert columns, page titles and characters into a worksheet.

Sub menu format is: Clear Direct Formating, Character, Paragraph, Bullets and Numbering, Page, Title Page, Change Case, Asian Phonetic Guide, Columns, Sections, Styles and Formating, AutoCorrect, Anchor, Wrap, Alignment, Arrange, Flip, Rotate, Group, Object, Frame/Object and Image.

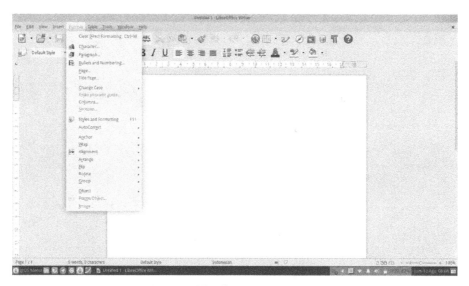

Picture 33: The Menu Format

Descriptions:

1. *Clear Direct Formatting*   Remove the direct formatting

2. *Character*   Insert the character into a worksheet

3. *Paragraph*   Set paragraphs in the document

4. *Bullets and Numbering*   Insert a bullet and numbering

5. *Page*   Set up a worksheet page

6. *Title Page*   Insert page title

7. *Change Case*   Change the shape of the case, example: *Uppercase* and *Lowercase*

8. *Asian Phonetic Guide*   Asian Phonetic keyboard Guide

9. *Columns*   Insert a column into a worksheet

10. *Sections*   Insert a section into a worksheet

11. *Styles and Formatting*   Insert styles and formatting

12. *AutoCorrect*   Enable word justification automatically on document

13. *Anchor*   Set the anchor to selected objects

14. *Wrap*   Enable wrap on a worksheet

15. *Alignment*   To set the alignment of the text in the document

16. *Arrange*   To set up the placement position objects on a worksheet, for example: above or behind text

17.	*Flip*	Reverse the position of the object, for example: vertical or horizontal
18.	*Rotate*	Rotate the position of the object
19.	*Group*	Combine several objects into one
20.	*Object*	Set the position and size of the objects in a worksheet
21.	*Frame/Object*	Insert an object/frame into a worksheet
22.	*Image*	Insert a picture into a worksheet

Each Sub Menu in Menu Format, has a Sub Sub Menu or options respectively. The following is a function of the options/Sub-Sub menus on the Sub Menu in the Menu Format.

Sub-Sub Menu Change Case

Sub's menu change case used to change the shape of the case. For example, you type a few sentences and you want the first letter of each sentence is capitalized, you can select options to Capitalize every word in the Sub Menu Change Case.

Sub's Menu Change Case is: Sentence Case, Lowercase, Uppercase, Capitalize Every Word, Toggle Case, Half Width, Full Width, Hiragana and Katakana.

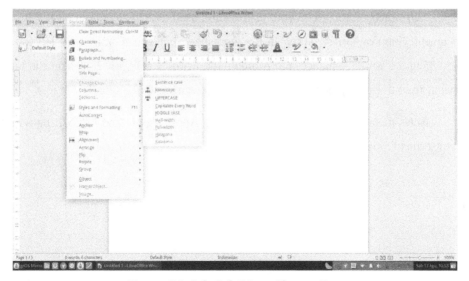

Picture 34: Sub-Sub Menu Change Case

Descriptions:

1. *Sentence Case* Change the characters into the beginning of each sentence capitalized

2. *Lowercase* Change capital letters into small letters on the document

3. *Uppercase* Change lowercase letters into uppercase in the document

4. *Capitalize Every Word* Change the character be capitalized at the beginning of each word

5. *Toggle Case* Change characters into toggle case

6. *Half Width* Change the selected Asian characters to half width characters

7. *Full Width* Change the selected Asian characters to full width characters

8. *Hiragana* Changing font Asian characters into Hiragana on a worksheet

9. *Katakana* Changing font Asian characters into Katakana on a worksheet

Sub-Sub Menu Autocorrect

Sub's menu autocorrect word justification used to activate automatically in the document. Suppose you're typing in the worksheet, but you momentarily led astray and typing the wrong sentence. For example the word ' I am ', to ' I a '. You can take advantage of this option is that it can reduce the occurrence of a typo.

Sub's menu autocorrect is: While Typing, Apply, Apply and Edit Changes and AutoCorrect Options.

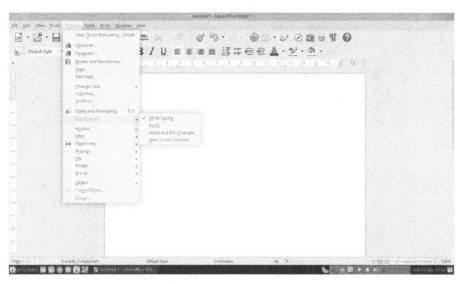

Picture 35: Sub-Sub Menu Autocorrect

Descriptions:

1. *While Typing*   Apply *auto correct* at the writing
2. *Apply*   Apply *auto correct* lineal
3. *Apply and Edit*   Apply and optional set *auto correct*
   Changes

Sub-Sub Menu Anchor

Sub's menu anchor serves to set the anchor to the selected object. Suppose you insert a picture into your worksheets and you want to put it into the Page (To Page), you can choose the option To Sub Menu Page in the Anchor.

Sub's Menu Anchor is: To Page, To Paragraph, To Character, As Character and to Frame.

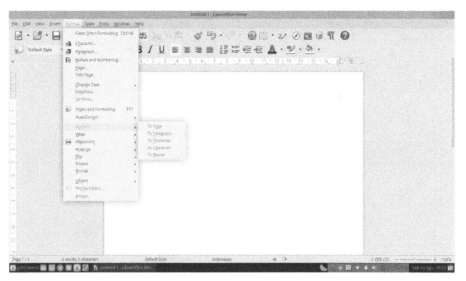

Picture 36: Sub-Sub Menu Anchor

Descriptions:

1. *To Page*   Put the anchor object into the page/pages
2. *In Paragraph*   Put the anchor object into paragraphs
3. *To Character*   Put the anchor object into characters
4. *As Character*   Put the anchor object as a character
5. *To Frame*   Put the anchor on the frame object

Sub-Sub Menu Wrap

Sub's menu wrap used to lay or set the position of the object (usually an image) on a worksheet. Suppose you want to put an image behind text or overwrite the text, you can use it easily due to LibreOffice Writer already provide it for you.

Sub's Menu Wrap is: Wrap Off, Page Wrap, Optimal Page Wrap, Wrap Through, In Background

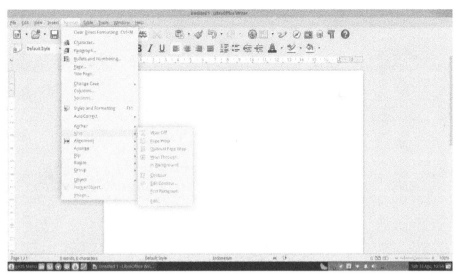

Picture 37: Sub-Sub Menu Wrap

Descriptions:

1.	*Wrap Off*	Me-off-right wrap on document
2.	*Page Wrap*	Positioning objects with Wrap to Page mode
3.	*Optimal Page Wrap*	Positioning objects with Optimal mode Page Wrap
4.	*Wrap Through*	Positioning objects with the Wrap mode Through
5.	*In Background*	Position of the object to the background
6.	*Contour*	Position of the object to the contours
7.	*Edit Contour*	Edit the settings of the contours on the document
8.	*First Paragraph*	Positioning objects on the first paragraph
9.	*Edit*	Changing font Asian characters into Katakana on a worksheet

Sub-Sub Menu Alignment

Sub's menu alignment is used to set the alignment of the text in the document. For example, you want the text to be left-align. You can select Align Left. You can also set text align right become align (Align Right), middle (Centered) and the mean left-right (Justified).

Sub's Menu Alignment is: Left, Right, Centered, Justified, Top, Center and Bottom.

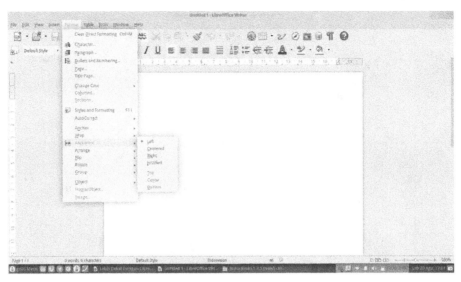

Picture 38: Sub-Sub Menu Alignment

Descriptions:

1.	*Left*	Make the text align left
2.	*Centered*	Make text centering
3.	*Right*	Make the text align right
4.	*Justified*	Make the text align left-right
5.	*Top*	Align text at the top of the selected objects
6.	*Center*	Align the text in the middle of the selected objects
7.	*Bottom*	Align the text at the bottom of selected objects

Sub-Sub Menu Arrange

Sub's menu arrange used to put the position of the object on a worksheet, for example: above or behind. For example, you want to put the pictures are in the rear position, you may select the option Send to Back on the Sub Menu Arrange. You can also put the object in front with select Bring to Front.

Sub's Menu Arrange is: Bring to Front, Forward One, Back One, Send to Back, To Foreground and To Background.

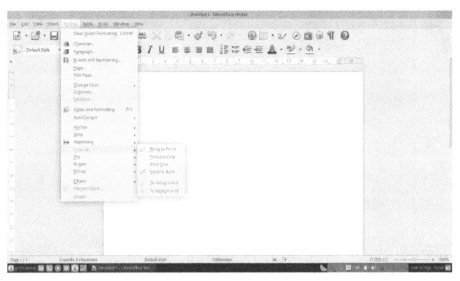

Picture 39: Sub-Sub Menu Arrange

Descriptions:

1. *Bring to Front*   Change the order of the selected object to the front

2. *Forward One*   Change the order of the selected objects is forwarded to the next

3. *Back One*   Change the order of the selected objects is forwarded to the back

4. *Send to Back*   Change the order of the selected object to the back

5. *To Foreground*   Change the order of the selected objects into the foreground

6. *To Background*   Change the order of the selected objects into the background

Sub-Sub Menu Flip

Sub's menu flip used to reverse the position of the object, for example: vertical or horizontal. Suppose you want to reverse the position of the picture from the horizontal into vertical. You can rotate it easily by selecting the option to Flip.

Sub Menu Flip is: Flip Vertically and Flip Horizontally.

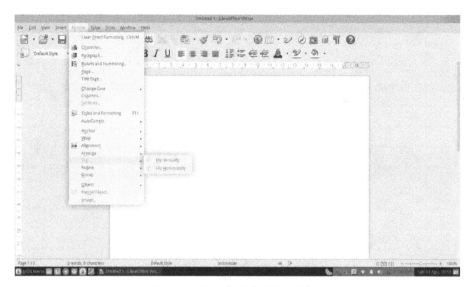

Picture 40: Sub-Sub Menu Flip

Descriptions:

1. Flip Vertically   Reverse the object vertically
2. *Flip Horizontally*   Reverse the objects horizontally

Sub-Sub Menu Rotate

Sub menus Rotate is used to rotate the object. Suppose you want to rotate the image of 90°-from the horizontal position becomes vertical. You can easily rotate it by using the Sub menus Rotate.

Sub's Menu Rotate is: Rotate 90° Left and Rotate 90° Right.

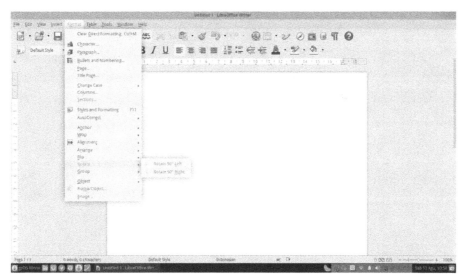

Picture 41: Sub-Sub Menu Rotate

Descriptions:

1. *Rotate 90° Left*   Rotate the object to the left direction of 90°
2. *Rotate 90° Right*   Rotate the object to the right direction of 90°

Sub-Sub Menu Group

Sub's menu group is used to combine several objects into one. Suppose you want to joins two separate images, you can easily combine it with select Rotate.

Sub's menu group is: Group, Ungroup, Enter Group and Exit Group.

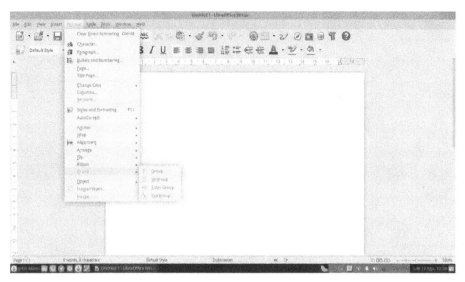

Picture 42: Sub-Sub Menu Group

Descriptions:

1. *Group*   Combine several objects into one
2. *Ungroup*   Undo Group
3. *Enter Group*   Opens the selected group, so you can edit the individual objects
4. *Exit Group*   Close the Group chosen, so that you cannot edit individual objects in a long time

Sub-Sub Menu Object

Sub Menu Object functions to set the position and size of the object into a worksheet. Suppose you want to edit the position and size of a picture that has been placed in a worksheet, you can easily set them up by selecting the option Position and Size.

Sub's Menu Object is: Position and Size, Line, Area, Text Attributes, Fontwork, Descriptions and Name.

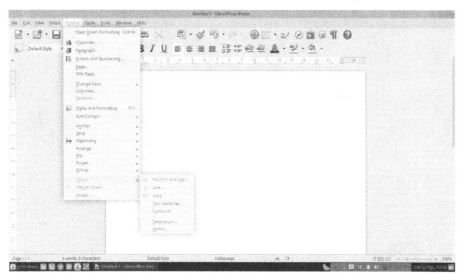

Picture 43: Sub-Sub Menu Object

Descriptions:

1. Position and Size   Set the position and size of the selected object
2. *Line*   Insert lines into documents
3. *Area*   Edit the object in your document area
4. *Text Attributes*   Inserts text into an object attribute
5. *Fontwork*   Fontwork insert into worksheets
6. *Descriptions*   Give a description on the object
7. *Name*   Naming objects

The Menu Table

Menu Table is used to create the chart, combining table, delete table, adding tables and inserts the formula (formula). Sub Menu Table: Insert, Delete, Select, Merge Cells, Split Cells, Protect Cells, Merge, Split Table, Table AutoFormat, AutoFit, Heading Rows Repeat, Convert, Sort, Formula, Number Format, the Table Boundaries and Table Properties.

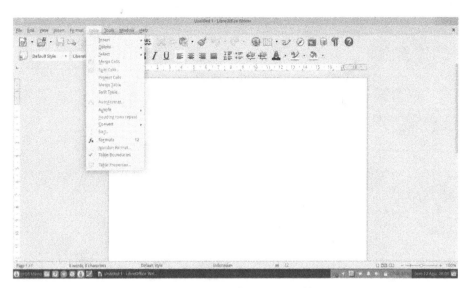

Picture 44: The Menu Table

Descriptions:

1. *Insert*   Insert a table in a document
2. *Delete*   Delete a table in a document
3. *Select*   Select the table in the document
4. *Merge Cells*   Merge the cells in the document
5. *Split Cells*   Separating the cells in the document
6. *Protect Cells*   Protect documents
7. *Merge Table*   Combining tables in documents
8. *Split Table*   Separate tables in documents
9. *AutoFormat*   Turn autoformat on the table
10. *AutoFit*   Turn autofit on the table
11. *Heading Rows Repeat*   Repeat row Headings from the table
12. *Convert*   Converting from text to a table or vice versa
13. *Sort*   Sort the contents of a table
14. *Formula*   Insert Formula (formula)
15. *Number Format*   Set aside the option selected from the formatting
16. *Table Boundaries*   Enable Table Boundaries
17. *Table Properties*   Enable Table Properties

Each Sub menu on the Table Menu, has a Sub Sub Menu or options respectively. The following is a function of the options/Sub-Sub Menu Sub Menu in the Menu on the Table.

Sub-Sub Menu Insert

Sub's menu insert is used to insert a chart into a spreadsheet/document Instance that you want to insert a table into the document, you can select the Insert option. Sub Sub Menu Insert, namely: Table Rows and Columns.

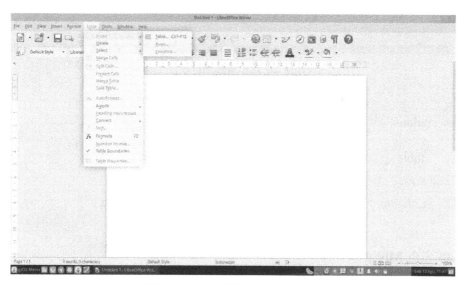

Picture 45: Sub-Sub Menu Insert

Descriptions:

1. *Table*   Insert a table into the document
2. *Rows*   Insert lines into documents
3. *Columns*   Insert a column into the document

Sub-Sub Menu Delete

Sub's menu delete used to delete tables, rows and columns in your document. You can use this feature to delete tables, rows and columns in your document with ease.

Sub's Menu Delete is : Table, Rows and Columns.

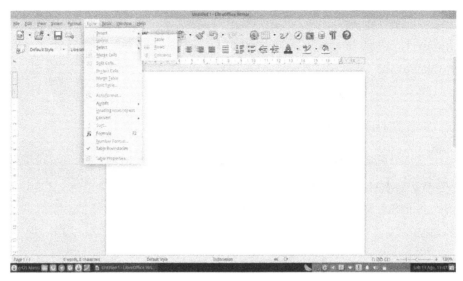

Picture 46 Sub-Sub Menu Delete

Descriptions:

1. *Table*   Delete a table in a document
2. *Rows*   Delete rows in the document
3. *Columns*   Remove the columns in a document

Sub-Sub Menu Select

Sub's menu select function to select a table, cell, row and column. For example, You want to choose a table, you can select the Table option on the Select Sub Menu.

Sub's Menu Select is: Table, Rows, Columns and Cells.

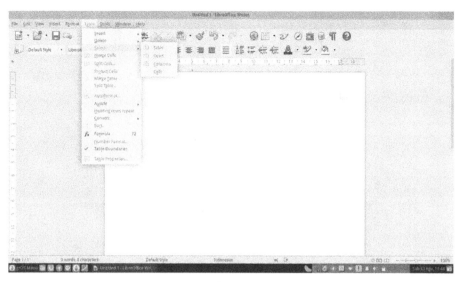

Picture 47: Sub-Sub Menu Select

Descriptions:

1.	*Table*	Selecting a table
2.	*Rows*	Selecting rows
3.	*Columns*	Selecting columns
4.	*Cells*	Selecting cells

Sub-Sub Menu AutoFit

Sub's menu autofit mode is used for the document. Suppose you want to set the column widths optimally, you can select the optimum mode of the Column Width.

Sub's menu autofit is: Column Width, Optimal Columns Width, Distribute Column Evenly, Row Height, Optimal Row Height, Distribute Row Evenly and Allow Row to Break Accross Pages and Columns.

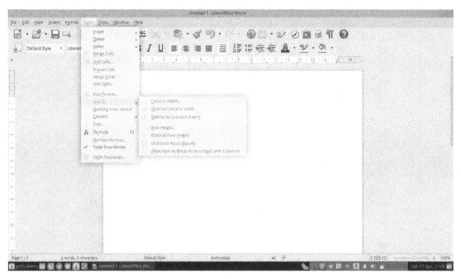

Picture 48: Sub-Sub Menu AutoFit

Descriptions:

1. *Column Width*   Set the width of a column
2. *Optimal Columns Width*   Set the width of the columns so that the optimal
3. *Distribute Column Evenly*   Set the columns evenly
4. *Row Height*   Set the height of row
5. *Optimal Row Height*   Set the height of the rows so that the optimal
6. *Distribute Row Evenly*   Set the height of the columns evenly
7. *Allow Row to Break Across Pages and Columns*   Allow the line to split between pages and columns

Sub-Sub Menu Convert

Sub's menu convert is used to change/convert text into a table or table into the text. With this option, you do not need to be complicated to change/convert the table into which you want.

Sub's Menu Convert is: Text to Table and Table to Text.

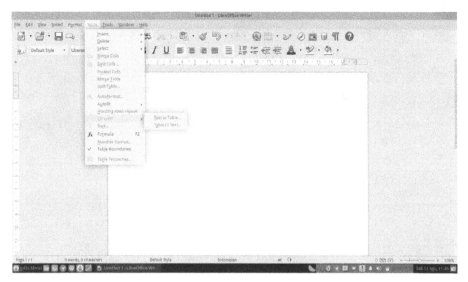

Picture 49:Sub-Sub Menu Convert

Descriptions:

1. *Text to Table*   Convert text into a table
2. *Table to Text*   Convert table to text

The Tools Menu

The tools menu serves to check spelling and grammar, count the number of words, insert a bibliography, mail merge, sorting, macro, auto correct, extension manager, customization and setting surrounding the LibreOffice Writer LibreOffice Writer.

Sub Menu Tools is: Spelling and Grammar, Language, Word Count, Outline Numbering, Line Numbering, Footnotes/Endnotes, Gallery, Bibliography Database, Address Book Source, Mail Merge Wizard, Sort, Calculate, Update, Macros, Extension Manager, XML Filter Settings, AutoCorrect Options, Customize and Options.

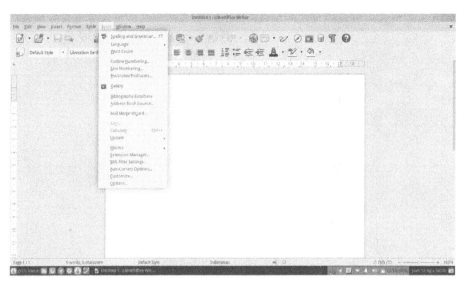

Picture 50: The Tools Menu

Descriptions:

1.	*Spelling and Grammar*	Check spelling and grammar
2.	*Language*	Select the default language to be used
3.	*Word Count*	Count the number of words
4.	*Outline Numbering*	Set the numbering on the worksheet
5.	*Line Numbering*	Set line numbering on a worksheet
6.	*Footnotes/Endnotes*	Insert a footnote.
7.	*Gallery*	Insert logos and symbols on the worksheet
8.	*Bibliography Database*	Insert a bibliography on a worksheet
9.	*Address Book Source*	Insert the source address book
10.	*Mail Merge Wizard*	Inserts a mail merge
11.	*Sort*	Set the order on documents alphabetically or numerically
12.	*Calculate*	Describe the setting calculation for numeric processing program
13.	*Update*	Update documents from previous changes
14.	*Macros*	Enable macro function
15.	*Extension Manager*	Manage extensions
16.	*XML Filter Settings*	Set the XML filter

17.	*AutoCorrect Options*	Set the AutoCorrect settings
18.	*Customize*	For customization LibreOffice Writer
19.	*Options*	Set the settings surrounding the LibreOffice Writer

Each Sub Menu in the Tools menu, has a Sub Sub Menu or options respectively. The following is a function of the options/Sub-Sub menus on the Sub Menu in the Tools Menu.

Sub-Sub Menu Language

Sub's menu language function to select the default language to use. The existence of this facility, the authors do not need to worry about the difficulty of the default language will be used. Because the LibreOffice Writer has been providing this option to facilitate the users.

Sub's Menu Language is: For Selection, For Paragraph, For All Text, Thesaurus, Hyphenation and More Dictionaries Online.

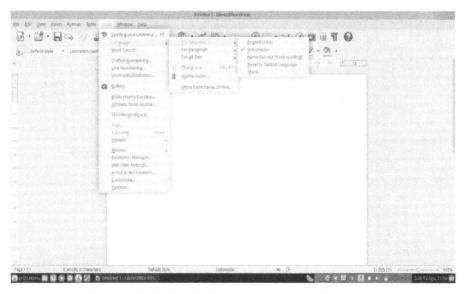

Picture 51: Sub-Sub Menu Language (For Selection)

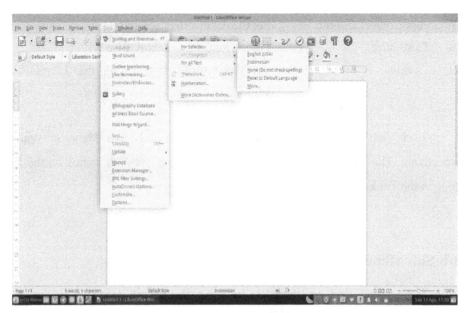

Picture 52: Sub-Sub Menu Language (For Paragraph)

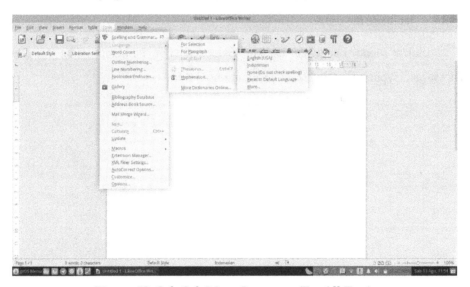

Picture 53: Sub-Sub Menu Language (For All Text)

Descriptions:

1. *For Selection*   Select the default language for selection

2. *For Paragraph*   Select the default language for paragraphs

3. *For All Text*   Select the default language for the entire text

4.	*Thesaurus*	Check each word with Dictionary Thesaurus
5.	*Hyphenation*	Separate the words with symbol separated.
6.	*More Dictionaries Online*	Check each word with another online dictionary

Sub-Sub Menu Update

Sub's menu update functions to update documents from previous changes. Suppose you want to update all documents or fields only. You can easily update it by choosing the option to Update All or Fields.

Sub's Menu Update is: Update All, Fields, Link, All Charts, Current Index, All Indexes and Tables and Page Formatting.

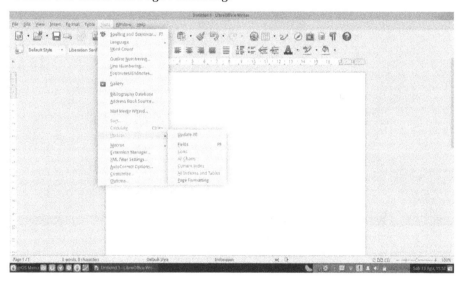

Picture 54: Sub-Sub Menu Update

Descriptions:

1.	*Update All*	Update the contents of the entire document
2.	*Fields*	Update the contents of a field
3.	*Link*	Update the link to the document
4.	*All Charts*	Update the entire diagram
5.	*Current Index*	To update a specific index

6.	*All Indexes and Tables*	Update the entire table and index
7.	*Page Formatting*	Update the settings page

Sub-Sub Menu Macros

The menu macros function to activate a function on LibreOffice Writer. Suppose you want to record the macro to do format, then any document you run the macro, the document will be formatted automatically according to your will. However, the average macro more utilized in LibreOffice Calc.

Sub's Menu Calc is: Record Macro, Run Macro, Organize Macros, Digital Signatures and Organize Dialogs.

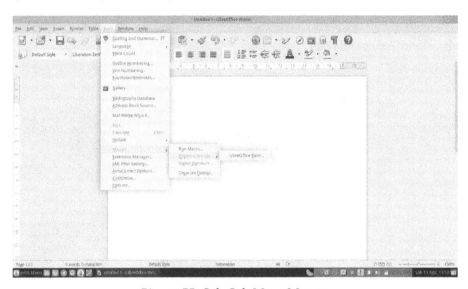

Picture 55: Sub-Sub Menu Macros

Descriptions:

1.	*Record Macro*	To record the activity into a macro
2.	*Run Macro*	To run the macro in the document function
3.	*Organize Macros*	To manage macro-macro on Writer
4.	*Digital Signatures*	Enable digital signatures
5.	*Organize Dialogs*	Manage Dialog Writer

By default, the Sub Menu Record Macros are not shown unless we turn on in advance via **Menu Tools Option >, then select Advanced > LibreOffice. Select the Enable macro recording (may be limited)**

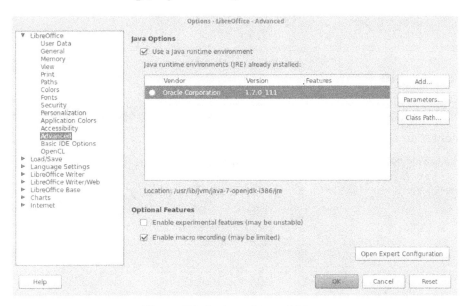

Picture 56: Activate Record Macro

Menu Window

Menu windows is used to open the same document and being active, close the active document and know the name of the document that is being worked on/off. Sub Menu Window IE: New Window and Close the Window.

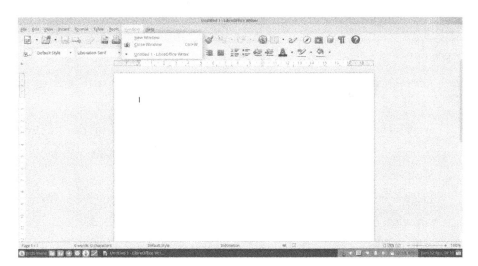

Picture 57: Menu Window

Descriptions:

1. *New Window*   Open the document that is active
2. *Close Window*   Close the active document

Menu Help

Menu help is used to ask for help about LibreOffice, send feedback, knowing information about license and LibreOffice. Sub Help Menu are: LibreOffice Help, what's This, Send Feedback, License Information and About LibreOffice.

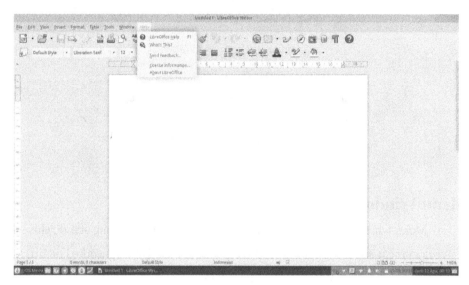

Picture 58: Menu Help

Descriptions:

1. *LibreOffice Help*   Find out information, functions and how to use tools-tools that exist on the LibreOffice
2. *What's This*   So users know the meaning one by one the icons and menus that are on the LibreOffice Writer
3. *Send Feedback*   Send feedback to libreoffice.org
4. *License Information*   To find out information from license LibreOffice
5. *Organize Dialogs About*   To find out information about LibreOffice, version
   LibreOffice   LibreOffice used, credit to libreoffice.org and

website of LibreOffice

BAB 6

HEADING

Copyright © 2016 Ade Malsasa Akbar < teknoloid@gmail.com >

Translated by Ilham Akbar <ilhamsahil05@gmail.com>

Heading

This chapter explains about how to compose the content in well structured arrangement, so that each component could be fully managed by the writer. A well structured arrangement could be achieved by applying a feature named *heading* (or called *Paragraph Style*) on the title, subtitles, and the sub of a writing subtitle. Benefits of using *heading* are so many, some of those are a full control of the whole article, the ease of arranging the index automatically and navigating (changing position) in a lengthy and complex article.

Applying Heading

Heading is commonly applied on the title, chapter title, subtitle, sub of a subtitle, etc. By applying *heading*, LibreOffice will record each *heading* as "one point" and it will fully map the document content into Navigator dialogue (F5).

- The way how to apply *heading* on **title** is by locating the cursor on the text > click *combo box* **Default Style** > select **Heading 1.**
- The way how to apply *heading* on subtitles is by locating cursor on the text > click *combo box* **Default Style** > select **Heading 2.**
- The way how to apply *heading* on the sub of a subtitle is by locating cursor on the text > click *combo box* **Default Style** > select **Heading 3.**

- Applying *heading* on **a sub of sub** is by doing the same step with a higher number. The deeper it is, the higher its number.

Quick Way: Shortcut for **heading 1** is **Ctrl+1**. *Shortcut* for **heading 2** is **Ctrl+2**. Shortcut for **heading 3** is **Ctrl+3**. The next *heading* only need the correct number.

Appearance of The Writing

The following figure is a simple document of which already have such a *heading* arrangement. Take a look on how the headings being applied, also take a look on the Navigator panel on the right side. The content of a document which already have *heading* will be mapped onto Navigator. Please compare with a document which has no *heading* at all (for example, just having **bold**).

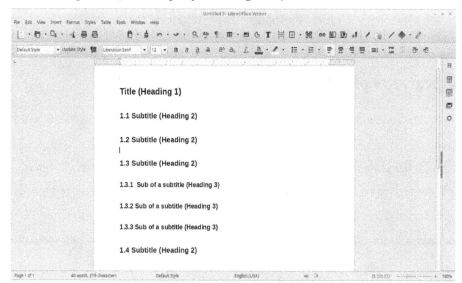

Picture 59: Heading Application

Appearance of Automatic Index

The following is the same document with an automatically created index. The result is tidy and consistent with the headings of which applied in advance/previous and surely matches with the map on the Navigator. In the other hand, the way how to create index lies on its specialized chapter.

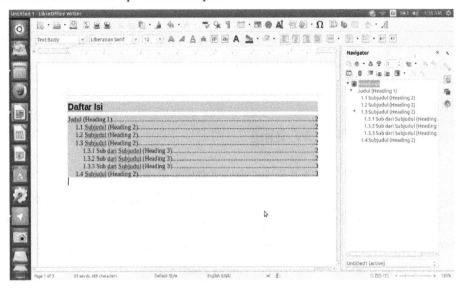

Picture 60: Appearance of Automatic Index

Appearance of PDF

The following figure is the appearance of the same document of which already saved as PDF file and shown on Evince document viewer application. That PDF file will have the same outline as it appears on a professional PDF file level. Of course its outline matches the heading arrangement of which already created, as match as in the Navigator, and matches the previous automatic index. Look onto the following Evince side-panel. In the other hand, the way how to create a PDF file lies on its specialized chapter.

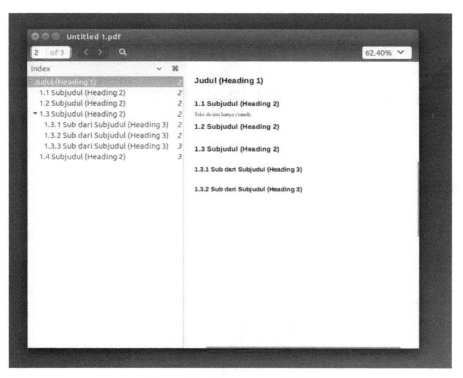

Picture 61: Appearance of PDF

CHAPTER 7

SHORTCUTS ON LIBREOFFICE WRITER

Copyright © 2016 Ade Malsasa Akbar <teknoloid@gmail.com>

Translated by Ilham Akbar <ilhamsahil05@gmail.com>

This chapter explains a number of commonly used shortcut keys for LibreOffice.

Shortcut	Function
Ctrl+A	To select the entire content of a document
Ctrl+O	To open a document of which already being saved once
Ctrl+S	To save the document
Ctrl+Shift+S	To save an active document with a different name of file
Ctrl+Alt+C	To create side comment box
Ctrl+F	To find a text or word
Ctrl+H	To find and replace a text or word
Ctrl+Z	To undo/cancel the previous command
Ctrl+Y	To redo the last canceled command
Ctrl+1	To apply heading 1
Ctrl+2	To apply heading 2
Ctrl+3	To apply heading 3
Ctrl+n	To apply heading n
Ctrl+N	To create a new document
Ctrl+W	To close a currently active document
Ctrl+C	To copy any selected object
Ctrl+V	To paste an already copied object into a document
Ctrl+Q	To close a currently active worksheet
Ctrl+E	Center text
Ctrl+R	Right align text
Ctrl+L	Left align text

Ctrl+J	Justify text
Ctrl+F2	To show Fields dialog box
Ctrl+F3	To show AutoText dialog box
Ctrl+F4	To close a currently active document/to save a document
Ctrl+F7	To show the Thesaurus tool
Ctrl+F10	To show Non-Printing Character
Ctrl+F11	To apply Paragraph Style
F1	To show LibreOffice Help center
F2	To show the toolbar of Formula
F5	To show Navigator
F7	To show Spelling management tool
F11	To show Styles and Formatting tool
F12	To apply numbering feature

Table 12: Shortcuts on LibreOffice Writer

CHAPTER 8
COMPATIBILITY

Translated by Mochammad Nur Afandi <localanu@gmail.com>

As we know, LibreOffice users in Indonesia are a bit and Mostly, computer users are using Microsoft Office for their Office Suite. It is difficult for beginner of LibreOffice while using LibreOffice. We have solutions for this problem mentioned in the list below:

LibreOffice Writer

- Using Nimbus Roman No.9 L for replacing Times New Roman font
- Using Nimbus Sans L for replacement of Arial font
- Saving document using pdf format or doc (Microsoft Office Document 2003) for reducing broken style in Microsoft Office Word

LibreOffice Calc

Saving document using xls format for avoiding compatibility issue on Microsoft Office Excel

LibreOffice Impress

Saving document using ppt format for avoiding compatibility issue on Microsoft Office PowerPoint. The best solution for this problem is using LibreOffice portable version from the portable devices and you can download it from https://www.libreoffice.org/download/portable-versions/.

CHAPTER 9

HOW TO WRITE ARABIC IN LIBREOFFICE WRITER

Copyright © 2016 Mukafi <kakafi30@gmail.com >

Translated by Raymon Rahmadhani <raymon.rahmadhani@gmail.com>

In the past, due to the limited sources, people got difficulties to write Arabic alphabet (Hijaiyah) using their computer. People used to write it manually If they want to do so. Nowadays, the need of using this kind of language is getting higher. Now, writing Arabic alphabet can be easily done in LibreOffice writer. Fortunately, LibreOffice facilitates tons of language writing types.

Therefore, the steps to type Arabic alphabet in LibreOffice Writer are as follows:

1. First, Make sure that you have added your keyboard characters.

Picture 62: Adding keyboard character

2. Then, add Arabic keyboard as shown in the following picture.

Picture 63: *Adding* Arabic type keyboard

3. Afterwards, Open your LibreOffice Writer application.

Picture 64: Default view of LibreOffice Writer

4. Click *"right to left"* menu on your LibreOffice writer.

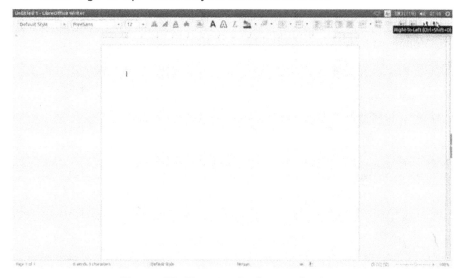

Picture 65: Choosing Right to Left Menu

By this way, Arabic alphabet can be typed in your LibreOffice. Furthermore, in order to type Arabic number, you may do the following steps:

5. Click the **Tools** menu. Then, choose **Options**.

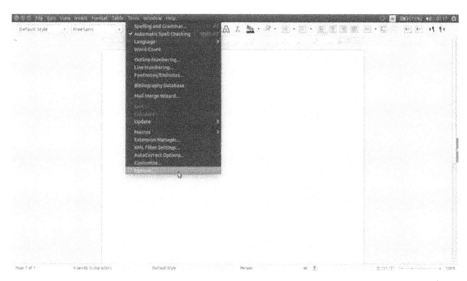

Picture 66: Choosing *option* in Tools menu

6. Then, go to **Language settings** and click **Complex Text Layout.** And then, go to **General Options** and change **Numerals** into **Hindi** as described in the following picture.

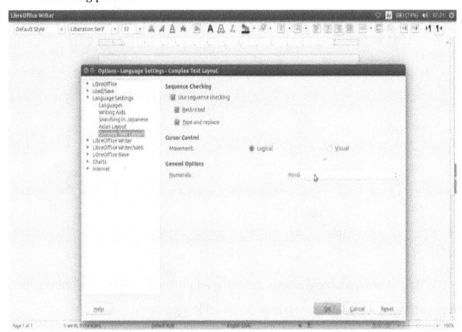

Picture 67: Changing *Numerals'* point to *Hindi*

7. The picture is the **screenshot** result.

Picture 68: A screen
shoot of Writing Arabic in LibreOffice Writer

CHAPTER 10

CREATING AN AUTOMATIC TABLE OF CONTENT

Translated by Raymon Rahmadhani <raymon.rahmadhani@gmail.com>

Table of content is important part that should be written in every paper, thesis, journal, etc. Therefore, it needs certain method to create it proper and neat. The following will be explained the steps that appropriate with LibreOffice Writer method to create it.

1. Firstly, the following picture is as the example.

Picture 69: Step 1 Creating an Automatic Table of Contents

2. Create a page for every sentence. Place the cursor at the beginning of the sentence, then press **Ctrl** + **Enter**. Pay attention to the following picture that describes how it goes.

Picture 70: Step 2 Creating an Automatic Table of Contents

3. Apply **heading** to the selected sentence in every created page that later on will help you to create the automatic Table of Contents. Apply level 1 **heading** (Heading 1) for the title, level 2 **heading** (Heading 2) for sub-title, and level 3 **heading** (Heading 3) for sub sub-title. As consideration, you have to apply it properly. Do not change the default font size given, changing the font size may cause the sentence does not emerge. Pay attention to the following picture.

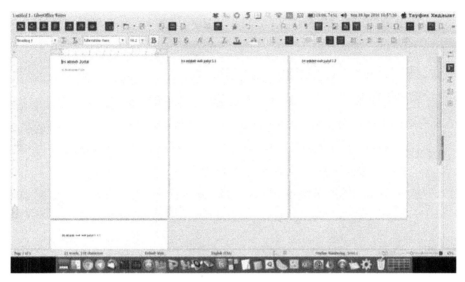

Picture 71: Step 3 Creating an Automatic Table of Contents

4. After applying the **heading**, create a new page which is placed before the title page you have created. It is prepared for Table of Contains page as described in the following picture.

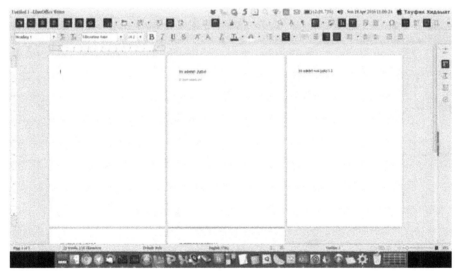

Picture 72: Step 4 Creating an Automatic Table of Contents

5. If all is ready, we can start creating the Table of Contents based on the following steps, those are clicking **Insert** at the tab menu for the first. Next, choose **Table of Contains and Index, then** choose **Table of Contents, Index or Bibliography.** Therefore, there will be a window as it's shown in the following picture.

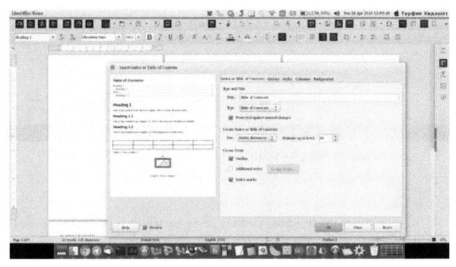

Picture 73: Step 5 Creating an Automatic Table of Contents

6. Leave empty or delete the sentence in Title column at Type and Title option as explained in the picture below.

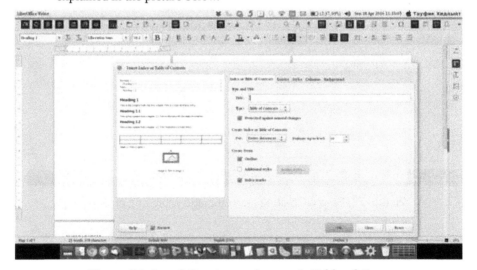

Picture 74: Step 6 Creating an Automatic Table of Contents

7. The following step is click OK. As the result, it will show as the following picture.

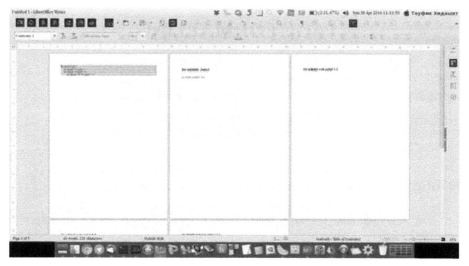

Picture 75: Step 7 Creating an Automatic Table of Contents

8. Finally, the steps of creating the automatic table of contents is complete. Additionally, as shown in the following picture, you may add a title above the table of contents and set the text position properly.

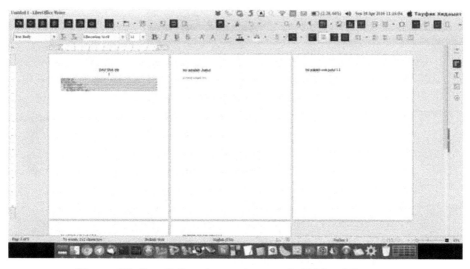

Picture 76: Step 8 Creating an Automatic Table of Contents

CHAPTER 11

PAGE FORMATTING

Translated by kucingsebelah <meongpus@hi2.in>

Setting Margins

In this Section, we will learn how to set Margins (edge of paper) in LibreOffice Writer, it is very simple

1. First at **Menu Bar** choose **Format** menu then select Page

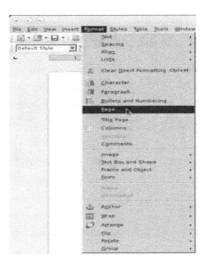

Picture 77: Setting Margins using **Format** Menu

2. **Window Page Style** menu will show up.
3. Choose **Paper Format** (A4, Letter, Legal or Longbond etc) then set the Margins size (Left, Right, Top, Bottom) and click **OK** button if you finish it.

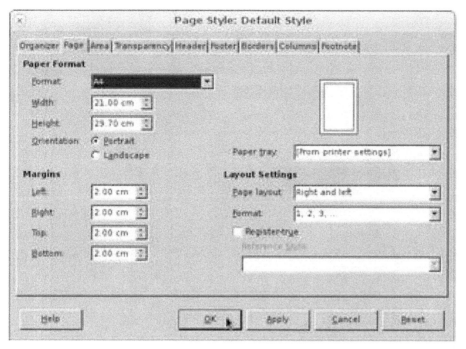

Picture 78: **Page Style** window

Advanced methods in setting up the Margins will explained in separate chapter.

Setting the Line Spacing

Line spacing is often used in reports, papers, report etc. Unfamiliar user may have difficulty to set the Line spacing. You can follow simple step as below:

1. First at Menu Bar choose Format **Menu** then **Paragraph.**

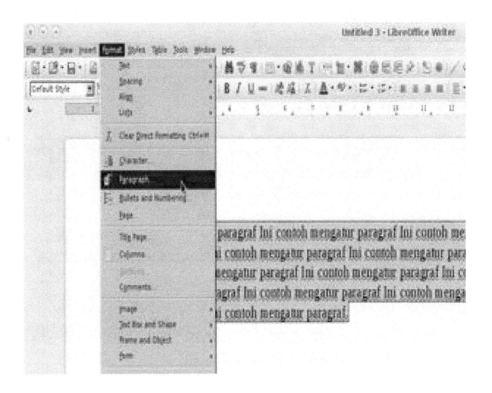

Picture 79: First step to setting *Line Spacing*

2. **Paragraph** window will show up.

3. At **Line Spacing** menu, choose spacing as you want (Single, 1.5 Lines, Double etc) then click **OK** button.

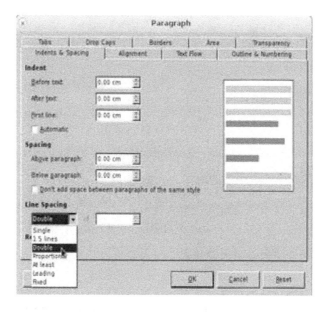

Picture 80 : *Paragraph* Window

In this tutorial, we implement ***Double spaces*** as example. Here's an illustration to simplify you getting the difference.

Before :

Picture 81: A Paragraph before using ***Double*** spaces

After :

Ini contoh mengatur paragraf Ini contoh mengatur paragraf Ini contoh mengatur paragraf Ini contoh mengatur paragraf Ini contoh mengatur paragraf Ini contoh mengatur paragraf Ini contoh mengatur paragraf Ini contoh mengatur paragraf Ini contoh mengatur paragraf Ini contoh mengatur paragraf Ini contoh mengatur paragraf Ini contoh mengatur paragraf Ini contoh mengatur paragraf Ini contoh mengatur paragraf Ini contoh mengatur paragraf Ini contoh mengatur paragraf Ini contoh mengatur paragraf.

Picture 82: A Paragraph after using *Double* spaces

Advanced methods to setting up the Line Spacing will explained in separated chapter.

Page Numbers

Page Numbers are very important part from a document, it simplify reader to search chapter or subsection. In Writer, a page number is a field that you can insert into your text.

To set up Page Numbers you can follow step as described below :

1. Choose **Insert** menu at Menu Bar.
2. Then choose **Header and Footer**, choose **Footer** sub-menu, then click **Default Style**.

Picture 83: how to set Page Numbers

3. A display will appear as below

Picture 84: Default Style from Sub Menu **Footer**

4. Enter the page number by selecting **Insert** menu → **Field** → **Page Number**. Automatically LibreOffice Writer will give the page number according to your page. By default, LibreOffice Writer will place the page number according to the documented alignment settings (left / align left / Ctrl + L). To make it at the right, you can use the right align right (Ctrl + R) command.

Picture 85: Page Number Menu

Picture 86: final result of **Page Number**

CHAPTER 12

INSERTING PICTURE

ON LIBREOFFICE WRITER

Copyright © 2016 Taufik Hidayat <yumtaufik1997@gmail.com >

Translated by Thoriq Kemal <thoriqcemal@gmail.com>

An Article will feels lack and bad if we can't find some picture inside of that. Explanation of some articles will be understood easily if we found some picture available. Therefore, reader will easily understand information from Article.

LibreOffice Writer has provided facilities to Insert Picture to the document since first release. Step by steps to Insert Picture on LibreOffice as below :

1. First Open your LibreOffice Applications.

2. Choose Menu **Insert** on Menu Bar.

Picture 87: Choose Insert Menu

3. Choose Sub Menu **Image**.

4. Then, there will be a dialog box like figure below.

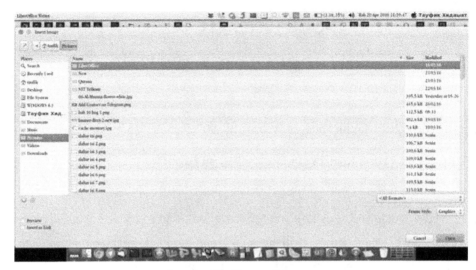

Picture 88: Choose Picture

5. Choose Picture which you will insert to document.

6. For Example of Picture which inserted to document, Look at figure below.

Picture 89: Picture which inserted to document

CHAPTER 13

CREATING TABLE ON LIBREOFFICE WRITER

Copyright © 2016 Taufik Hidayat <yumtaufik1997@gmail.com >

Translated by Thoriq Kemal <thoriqcemal@gmail.com>

We often find some articles or information which is excessive and complicated. This can make us bored before we finish to read it. By using Table, some explanations and illustration can be summarized to data arrangement. The figure below is an example of Table we quoted from the internet.

Tabel Struktur Penduduk Jawa Tengah
menurut Golongan Umur Tahun 2000-2003

Golongan Umur	Tahun 2000	Tahun 2001	Tahun 2002	Tahun 2003
<1	470.699	528.153	518.118	870.244
1 - 4	2.007.647	2.148.007	2.169.159	1.692.242
5 - 14	6.219.667	6.279.900	6.332.011	6.288.873
15 - 44	14.914.069	14.791.458	15.123.085	15.452.356
45 – 64	5.269.177	5.353.495	5.533.490	5.686.550
65 ke atas	1.894.587	1.962.805	2.016.003	2.062.575
Total	30.775.846	31.063.818	31.691.866	32.052.840

Sumber : BPS. Propinsi Jawa Tengah, Hasil Pengolahan Susenas 2003 dan Data Profil Kesehatan Kab/Kota di Jateng yang telah konfirmasikan dengan BPS Propinsi Jawa Tengah untuk tahun sebelumnya

Picture 90: Example Table[1]

---

1   http://acciejie.blogspot.co.id/2013/03/membaca-grafik-tabel-dan-bentuk.html diakses pada 22 Juli 2016

Step by step to create Table:

1. First Open your LibreOffice Application.

2. Further, on Menu Bar Click **Table,** Look at figure below.

Picture 91: Choose Table on Menu Bar

3. Choose **Insert Table** or keyboard shortcut **Ctrl+F12**.

4. Insert Table Name, Columns and Rows. Look at the figure below.

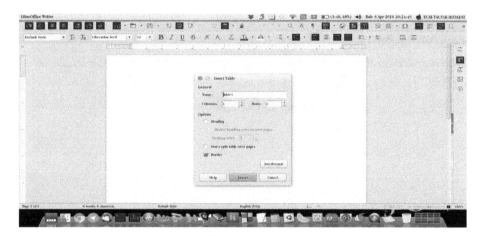

Picture 92: Insert Table Name, Columns and Rows

5. Click **Insert** to Insert Table.

6. Then will display like figure below.

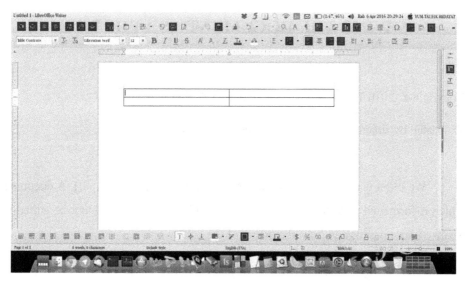

Picture 93: Results from Insert Table

Notes:

You can add, edit or delete table accordance with your needs.

CHAPTER 14

SAVING THE DOCUMENT AS A PDF FILE

Copyright © 2016 Taufik Hidayat <yumtaufik1997@gmail.com >

Translated by Ilham Akbar <ilhamsahil05@gmail.com>

We often use a document of which formatted as PDF file (.pdf). A document which is formatted as PDF is more secure from virus attack and cannot be edited so easily without permission from the owner of the data.

To save a document as PDF file on LibreOffice Writer is trivial, because the procedure is similar with the step of saving a document. The difference is the choice of document saving format.

There are two different methods to save a document into PDF format.

Method 1:

1. First, prepare the document.

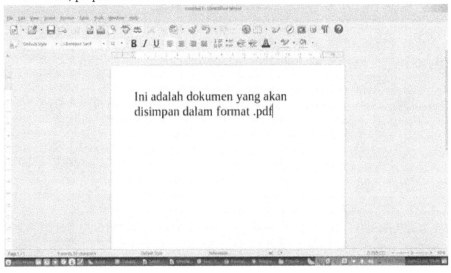

Picture 94: A Sample of Document Which Will be Saved Into PDF Format

2. Click **File** on the Menu Bar.

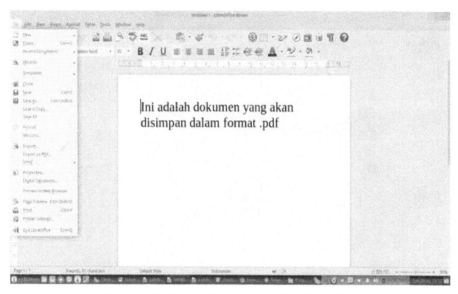

Picture 95: Select File Menu on The Menu Bar

3. Select its sub-menu named **'Export as PDF'**.

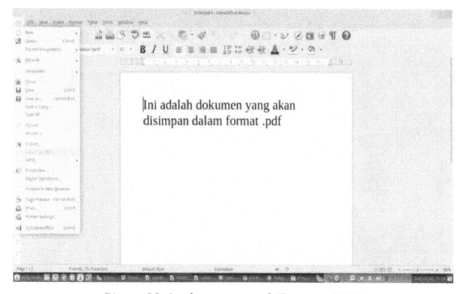

Picture 96: A sub-menu named 'Export as PDF'

4. After that, a **PDF Options** window will appear. We can set how the appearance of our PDF file will be. Click **Export** button to start export process.

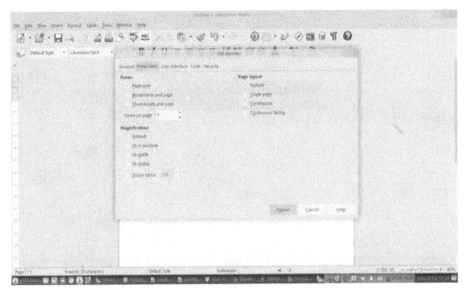

Picture 97: A sub-menu named 'Export as PDF'

5. On the Export window, input the document name and set the purpose of saving the document. Click **Save** to finish.

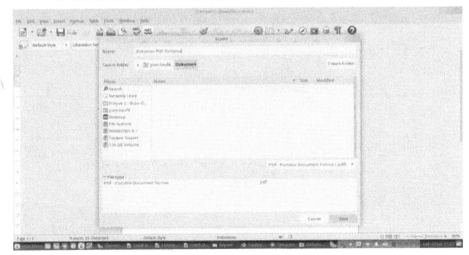

Picture 98: Export Window Appearance

6. The following image is the result of the document of which saved into PDF format.

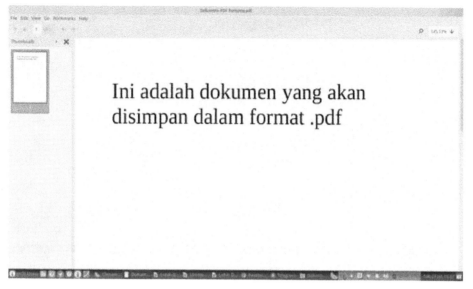

Picture 99: PDF Viewer Software Showing The Document

Method 2:

1. Prepare the document of which will be saved into PDF format.

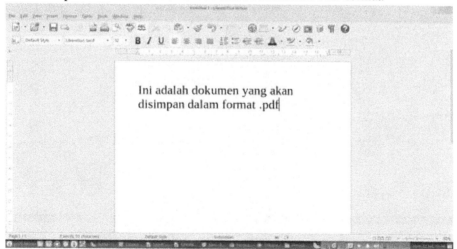

Picture 100: A Sample of The Document of which Will be Saved Into PDF Format.

2. Next, click the icon of **'Export Directly as PDF'** on the *toolbar*.

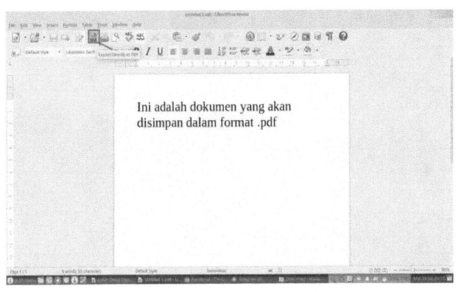

Picture 101: Logo Export Directly as PDF shown by pointing cursor

3. The Export window will appear. Input the document name and select where will the document be saved.

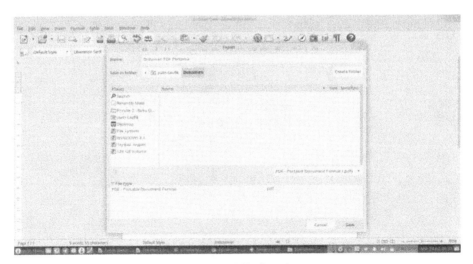

Picture 102: Export Window Appearance

4. Finally, this is the document which is saved into PDF format

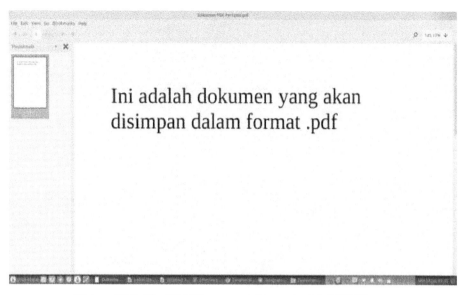

Picture 103: The PDF Document Opened with PDF Viewer

CHAPTER 15

INSERTING HEADER AND FOOTER

IN LIBREOFFICE WRITER

Copyright © 2016 Sasongko Bawono <sasongko262@gmail.com>

Translated by Faiq Aminuddin <dampuawang@gmail.com>

Inserting Header

Usually, there is a header in the top of letter, book etc. There are three ways to add the header to the document;

First Way:

1. First, click above the top of the text area above margin.

Picture 104: Step 1 Inserting Header

2. Next, click Header (Default Style).

Picture 105: Step 2 Inserting Header

3. If the cursor have moved to the Header area, add a sentence or words as a header.

Picture 106: Step 3 Inserting Header

Second Way:

1. First, click **Insert menu** on Menu Bar

2. Next, select **Header menu** and choose **Default Style**.

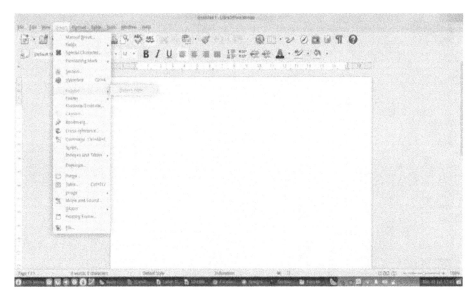

Picture 107: Step 1 and 2 for Inserting Header

3. If the cursor have moved to the header area, you can write a sentence or words as the header.

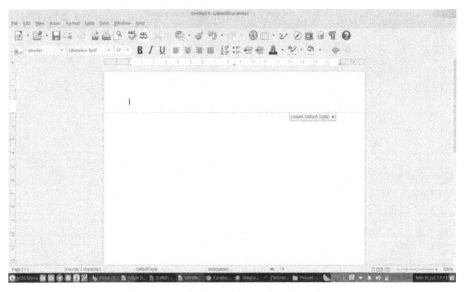

Picture 108: Step 3 Inserting **Header**

Third Way:

1. First, click Format menu on **Bar Menu.**
2. Next, click **Page Menu**.

Picture 109: Step 1 and 2 for Inserting **Header**

3. On Page Style window, click **Header tab**, then click check box on **Header on**, then click **Apply button**.

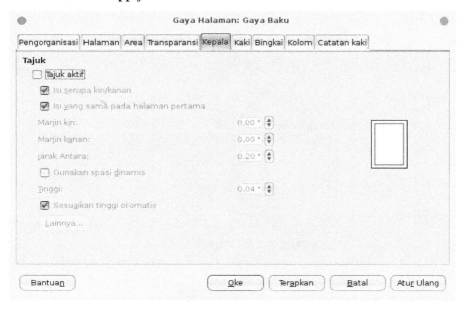

Picture 110: Step 3 Inserting **Header**

4. Click on top part of document area, then add the header.

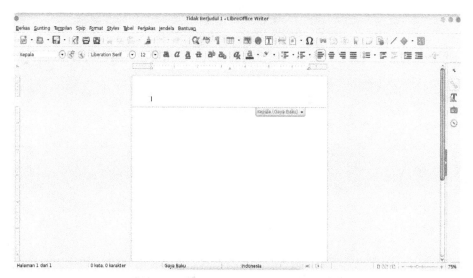

Picture 111: Step 3 Inserting **Header**

Removing Header

A header can be removed easily. We can remove the header directly or from the menu bar. There are two ways to removing header from document page. The ways are;

First Way:

1. First, click the header directly.

Picture 112: Step 1 Removing header

2. Next, click the **Header (Default Style)**, then click **Delete Header**.

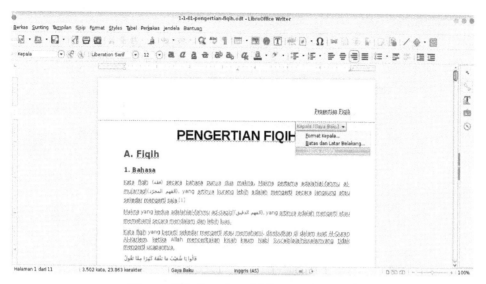

Picture 113: Step 2 and 3 Removing Header

3. Finally, when confirmation window appear, click Yes.

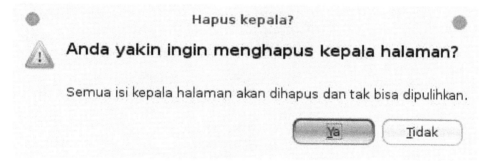

Picture 114: Confirmation window for removing header

Second Way:

1. First, click Format on Menu Bar.

2. Next, click Page.

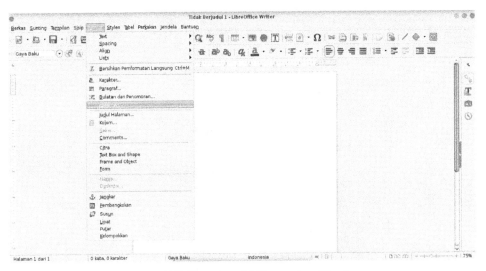

Picture 115: Step 1 and 2 Removing **Header**

3. Next, when Page Style window appear, click Header tab for removing the **header**.

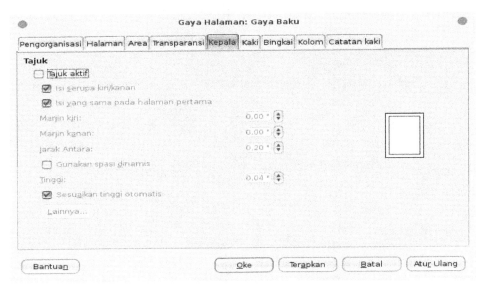

Picture 116: Step 3 Removing **Header**

4. Click the **Header on check** box for removing the check sign.

5. 5. Finally, click **OK**.

Inserting Footer

A footer is a text as a page number which always appear on bottom part of document. A footer is similar to a header. The difference between footer and header is its place. The header is on top part of document, while the footer is on bottom part of document.

Similar to inserting header, there are three ways in inserting footer;

Firs Way:

1. First, click on bottom part of document.

2. Next, click **Footer (Default Style) +**.

Picture 117: Step 1 and 2 Inserting Footer

3. Then, look at the cursor that moved. It indicate that the footer is active. Next, write a word or a sentence as a footer of your document.

Picture 118: Step 3 Inserting Footer

Second way:

1. First, click **Format** on the Menu Bar.

2. click **Page**.

Picture 119: Step 1 and 2 Inserting Footer

3. Click **footer tab**, then click **the Footer on check box**. Click **Apply** to apply the footer. Klik tab **Kaki/Footer**.

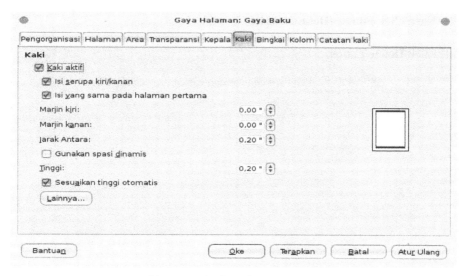

Picture 120: Step 3 Inserting Footer

4. Finally, click button OK.

Removing Footer

A Footer can be removed easily. There are two ways for removing footer;

1. First, click **the footer**

Picture 121: Step 1 Removing Footer

2. Next, click **Footer (Default Style).**

3. Click **Delete Footer**.

Picture 122: Step 2 and 3 Removing Footer

4. Then, when confirmation window is appearing, click Yes for removing the footer.

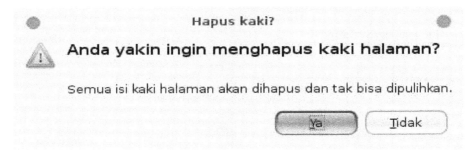

Picture 123: Step 4 and 5 Removing Footer

Second Way:

1. First, click Format on Menu Bar. Then, click Page.

Picture 124: Step 1 Removing Footer

2. click **footer tab**.

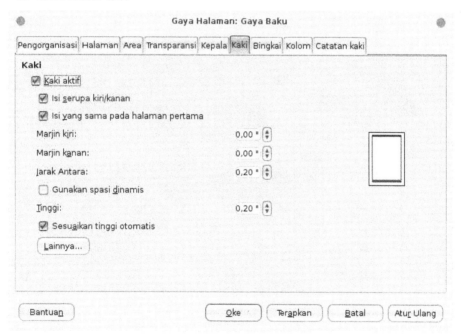

Picture 125: Step 2 Removing Footer

3. Then, click **Footer on check box**. So, the check is gone. Click **OK**.

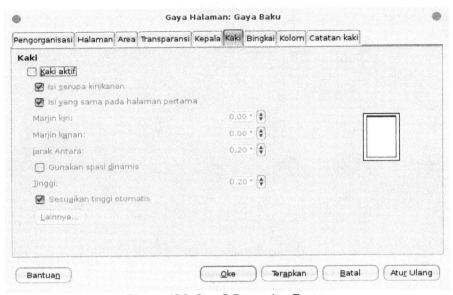

Picture 126: Step 3 Removing Footer

CHAPTER 16

SAVING DOCUMENT

After typing a document, we need to save it so we can edit it again. There are two common methods ie. **Save** and **Save As**. **Save** is used to store documents with same name and location while **Save As** is used to store documents with different name, location or formats.

A. Saving Document Using "Save" and "Save As" from "File" Menu

1. First choose "**File**" menu

2. Choose "**Save**" to store document with the same name and location or choose "**Save As**" to store document with different name, location or formats. If we choose "**Save As**" a window menu will appear, fill the name of document, choose new file location or change document format then click "**Save**"

Picture 127: Saving document using **"Save"**

Picture 128: Saving document using **"Save As"**

B. Saving Document Using Save Button

You can click save button (Floppy Disk logo on left Toolbar) to save document. To Save As, you can click drop down / black triangle logo (right side of Floppy Disk logo) then, choose "**Save As**". Window menu will appear, fill the name of document, choose new file location or change document format then click "**Save**"

C. Saving Document Using Keyboard Shortcut

You can also use keyboard combination key to save the document, by pressing **Ctrl + S** to save document or press **Ctrl + Shift + S** to Save As document (a window menu will appear then you can fill new name, location or format).

D. Saving Document Automatically

You can save the document automatically with interval time :

1. First, click the "**Tools**" menu on the Menu Bar.
2. Then choose "**Options**" menu.

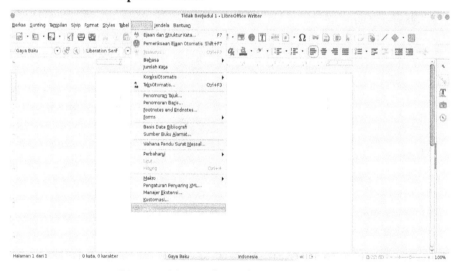

Picture 129: "**Tools**" and "**Option**" Menu

3. "**Options**" windows will appear.

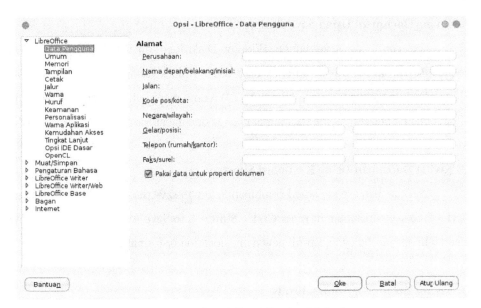

Picture 130: Libre Office "**Option**" Window

4. then choose "**Load/Save**" sub menu

5. choose "**General**"

6. In the "**Save**" section, check "**Save AutoRecovery information every**" option then fill the time interval (in minutes) after that, click **OK / OK**.

Picture 131: setting automatically saving the document

CHAPTER 17

MAKING LINE SPACING ON LIBREOFFICE WRITER

Copyright © 2016 Taufik Hidayat <yumtaufik1997@gmail.com >

Translated by Astrida Atni Ayu Mahardini <astriddini7@gmail.com>

Line spacing functions to set the spacing between lines/distance. Line spacing is the distance between the lines of text that are above or below. Generally, *line spacing default value* is *1 (single)*. However, we can organize them into a *1,5* or *2 (double)*. *Line spacing* is indispensable for the making of: term papers, theses, manuscripts, theses, etc.

Below are the steps to make line spacing on LibreOffice Writer, that is as follows.

Method 1:

1. First, create the first paragraph will be given the **line spacing.**

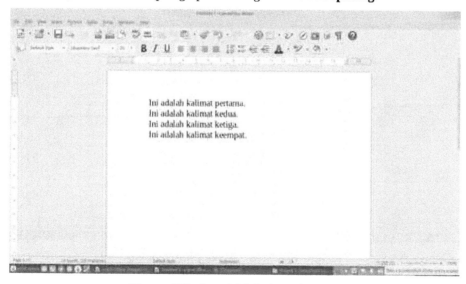

Picture 132: Step 1 Make Line Spacing

2. Next, select entire sentence that is already completed.

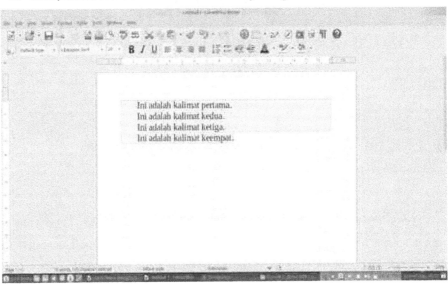

Picture 133: Step 2 Make *Line Spacing*

3. Next, click the Format menu on the Menu Bar and highlight the Paragraphs. It will pop up a window display Paragraphs.

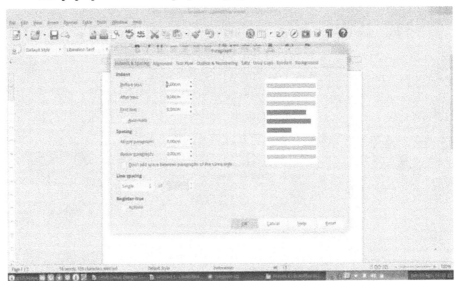

Picture 134: Step 3 Make *Line Spacing*

4. Select **the tab Indent & Spacing**. On the choice of Line Spacing, please choose the size of the line spacing you want. As for the line spacing is provided: **Single, 1.5 Lines, Double Proportional, At Least, Leading and Fixed.**

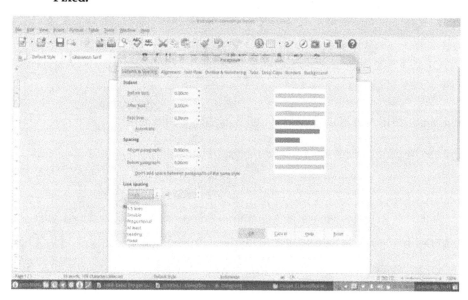

Picture 135: Step 4 Make Line Spacing

5. Lastly, this is the result of **line spacing**. In this case, it uses **the line spacing 1.5.**

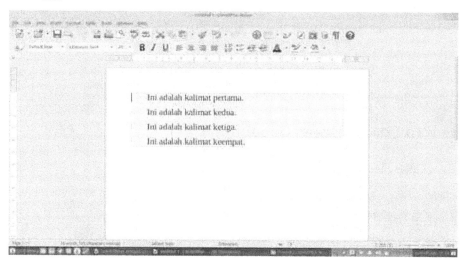

Picture 136: Step 5 Make *Line Spacing*

CHAPTER 18

FIND AND SMART REPLACE WITH

REGULAR EXPRESSION

Translated by Astrida Atni Ayu Mahardini <astriddini7@gmail.com>

Find & Replace feature in LibreOffice Writer has been equipped with the capabilities of the regular expression. With these capabilities, search and replace text became very sophisticated without limits. For those of you who are unfamiliar with this feature, regular expression (regex) is a method which is standardized internationally to improve discovery of patterns in text1. The regex has been applied on all types of software; for example in Office suite, in the search engines (including Google), and of course on each of your operating system.. With a regex, you can perform text searches more efficiently. Amazingly enough, the regex is studied in one piece of software then it can be applied in all other software. This chapter will show you two examples of the use of the regex.

How To Enable Regex Capabilities

Open the Find dialog & Replace (Ctrl + H) and then check the options of Regular Expression or by selecting the Edit Menu on the Menu Bar and then highlight the option Find & Replace.

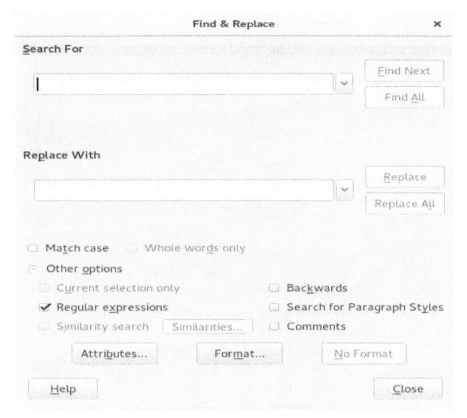

Picture 137: Enable Regex Capabilities

Example 1

You have a text document containing 10,000 rows in the beginning of each row there is a line number. How do You delete only the line number in front of it for 10,000 lines of text? If you delete it manually, it's very tiring and time wastes. If you do it with regular expression, you can delete everything in second

Regular expression:

```
^[0-9]*[0-9].
```

Demonstration:

Picture 138: Demonstration Example 1 (Before)

Picture 139: Demonstration Example 1 (After)

Explanation of example 1:

Regular expression that reads ^ [0-9] * [0-9]. It actually consists of 3 parts:

1. The first part is the ' ^ ' (radical written) which meant the beginning of the line. This character searches for the earliest part of the targeting of each row (because the line number to be there).

2. The second part is ' [0-9] * [0-9] ' which means any kind of digits, starting with the number [0-9] and end with a number [0-9]. This regular expression will be targeting figures ranging from 0 to 10000, even up to unlimited. As for the character ' * ' in the middle is the cause of this regular expression equates how many digits.

3. The third part is a '. ' (a dot character) which means that any one character. In the example of the use of the regular expression, the dot character represents one space between line number and the name of the OS that is always there in every line.

4. The workings of the regular expression in the Find/Replace this overall & is focusing the target to the beginning of the line first, then matching the number of how many digits, and then matching one character space, and replacing it with a blank character (the same as delete), and then repeating it until the end of the document. The result is all line numbers removed.

Example 2

You have a text document that contains 10,000 lines of text that are on the sidelines between one with another line there is one empty line without text. How to remove the entire blank lines so that only the text lines are left? If you do it manually, then this takes very long and tiring. But with regular expression, you can do it in the blink of an eye.

Regular expression:

Demonstration:

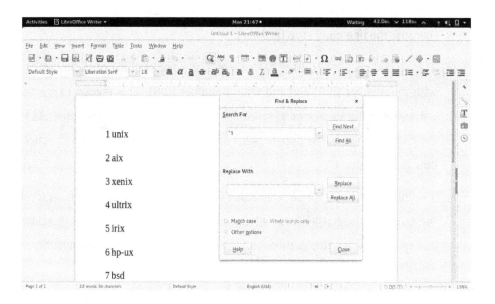

Picture 140: Demonstration Example 2 (Before)

Picture 141: Demonstration Example 2 (After)

Explanation Example 2 :

Regular expression used here is a `^$`. The first part is the `^` (Caret Character) which means the beginning of the line. The second part is a `$` (Dollar Character) meaning the end of the line. The combined regular expression `^$` means the beginning of a line, end of line without any text,   which is tantamount to an empty row. This Regular expression searches for every blank line. If replacement/replace with was left blank, then replace the activity will delete all blank lines in the text.

Advanced Reference:

See the following references If you want to be more steeped in the regular expression. http://www.regular-expressions.info is website that gives information source regular expression with very good and complete.

- http://www.regular-expressions.info/examples.html presents real examples of regular expression.

- Https://www.wikibooks.org/wiki/Regular_Expressions/POSIX-Extended_Regular_Expressions presents tables code regular expression and its meaning from WikiBooks.

CHAPTER 19

MAIL MERGE IN LIBREOFFICE WRITER

Translated by Astrida Atni Ayu Mahardini <astriddini7@gmail.com>

Mail merge is a facility to facilitate the making of letters available on the document processing devices. Mail merge is used to specify a list of recipients that are stored on a database created previously in the document we made, so we just need to make a letter as a template and recipients will be listed automatically.

The steps in the mail merge LibreOffice Writer include:

1. Prepare the template document and *database* of recipients.

2. Insert the receiver into the database mail.

3. Save and print the results of a *mail merge*.

Preparing the Template Document and Database Receiver

We create a document in LibreOffice Writer (can either be letters, invitations, Charter or certificate, or other), as the following example.

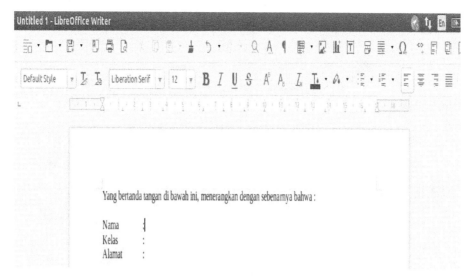

Picture 142: Template Document for *Mail Merge*

Finished preparing form letters, we create a database of recipients. This receiver can be a database table spreadsheet, text file or database. However, in the discussion of this time, we use the spreadsheet table as the source of its data, because this is the most common way and easy to use.

We make tables of recipients in LibreOffice Calc. We make sure our content stands on the first line of the Header Column, and the list of recipients we put on the second line, like the example below.

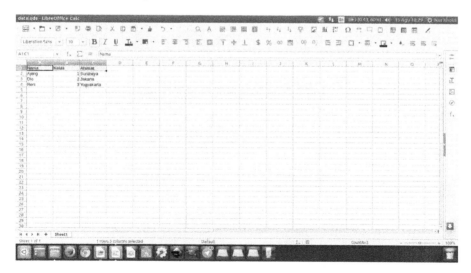

Picture 143: List Of Recipients Using LibreOffice Calc

After that, we save the file. Until this stage, the first step has been completed.

Inserting the receiver into the Mail Database

The next step is we open the file letter we made on LibreOffice Writer above, we then select Edit > Exchange Database... it will pop up a dialog as shown below.

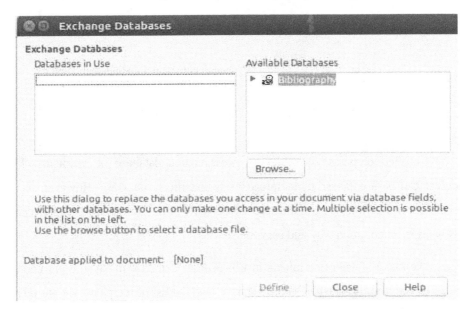

Picture 144: *Template* Document for *Mail Merge Template*

Press the **Browse** button and select **the spreadsheet** we have made earlier. After that, it will appear a new database from the list of **existing databases**. Double click the new database we paste, select the **sheet** that contains the data that we have to prepare, and then click **Define** like the illustration below.

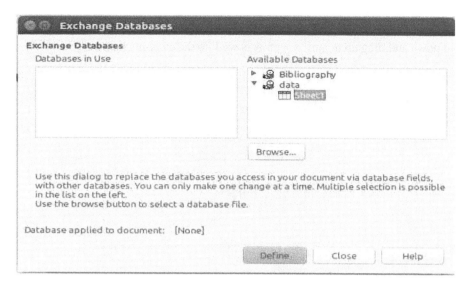

Picture 145: Selecting The Database

Next is click **View** > **Data Sources** or press **Ctrl+Shift+F4** to display form Data Sources, select **the database** that we have created above, click Tables, and then select the name of the table that we have to prepare in advance. In General, this table name based on the name of the Sheet in the file that we created.

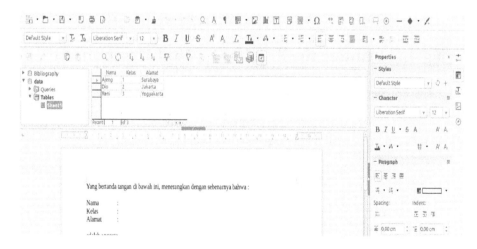

Picture 146: displaying a list receiver of **Data Sources**

As shown above, after we open the Sheet1 data we have made earlier will appear in **the Data Sources**. The next step is to connect **the database** to document letter by draging and droping on the name of the field. Click the name of the column, hold down and drag up to stuff documents we like the example below.

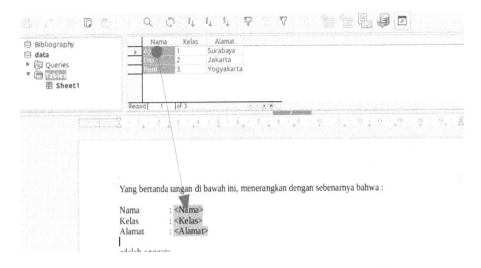

Picture 147: Drag and Drop from the Data Sources into your document

As such, we've finished pasting the list of recipients into the template document.

Saving and Printing the Results of a *Mail Merge*

The last step is to save and print the results of a mail merge. The trick is to open the *mail merge* dialog via **the Tools menu** > **Mail merge Wizard...** or by clicking the icon in the mail merge **Data Source** while displaying.

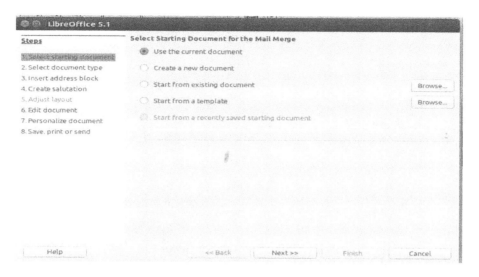

Picture 148: *Mail Merge Wizard*

To save and print a document the results of the mail merge, we can skip directly to step number 8.

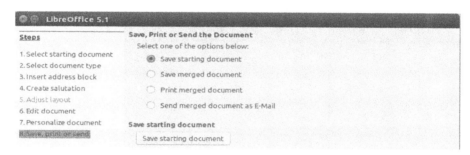

Picture 149: *Save, print or send* in *Mail Merge*

So far, it can be adapted to our desires. If we choose the Save **starting document**, it will be created a new document with the results of *the mail merge*. If we choose **Save merged document**, then we are given three options, namely **the Save as single document** to store all the results of **the mail merge** into a single file, **Save as individual documents** to save to multiple files, and **From ... To ...** to save some of the results of the mail merge to multiple files.

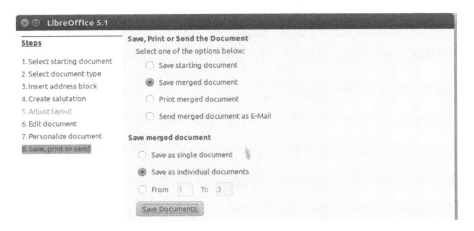

Picture 150: *Save Merged Document*

To print the results of *the mail merge*, select the '**Print merged document**', then it would appear the option Properties for the printer settings, **Print all document** to print the entire document *mail merge*, and **From ... to ...** to print some of the **mail merge** results.

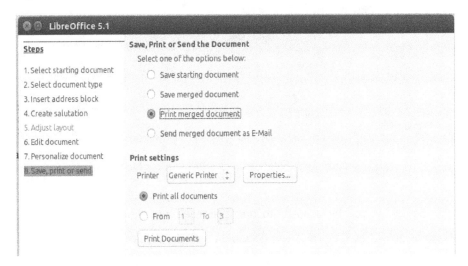

Picture 151: Print merged document

If the recipient list is an email address, we can send you the mail merge results to existing addresses in the recipient list.

Once completed, we click Finish to close the Mail merge Wizard. As such, we've managed to do a mail merge on LibreOffice Writer.

CHAPTER 20

EYE PROTECTION PAPER IN

LIBREOFFICE WRITER

Copyright © 2016 Aziz Rahmat Pratama <azis.pratama@gmail.com>

Translated by Azis R. Pratama <azis.pratama@gmail.com>

By default, LibreOffice Writer does not have "Eye Protection Mode" feature, like WPS Office. But don't worry, with a little trick and creativity, user can still modify the plain white paper into more healthy green color.

The advantage of this little tweak is to reduce eye-strain effect, when the writer must work long hours duration, in front of his/ her monitor screen. This is the end result of "eye protecting paper" after the theme successfully being applied.

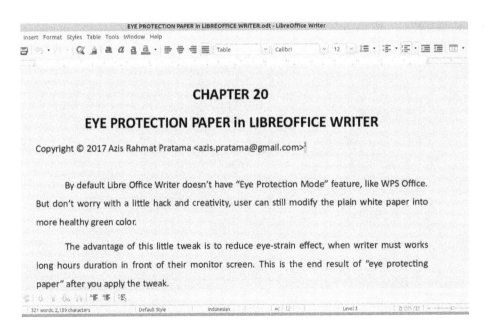

Picture 152: **#C7EDCC** Eye-Protection Paper in Libre Office Writer.

Don't worry, this tweak only affect your LibreOffice on your computer, even after apply this configuration, you can still print the hard-file and share the soft-file without being worry about the paper color. So, consider this tweak. It is kind of tweaking your LibreOffice suite. Currently, I'm using LibreOffice version 5.4.0.3

Picture 153: LibreOffice 5.4.0.3

Technically, there are some different configuration between the current LibreOffice and the older version. In the older version of LibreOffice, there are some additional steps to define new color scheme. But, it seems in then current version, the **color** and the **application color** configuration is merged. Alright, here is the step by step to apply "Document Background" color in LibreOffice 5.4.0.3 or above/ newest version.

1. Open **Tools** menu, and then pick sub menu **Option (ALT+F12)**, for keyboard shortcut.

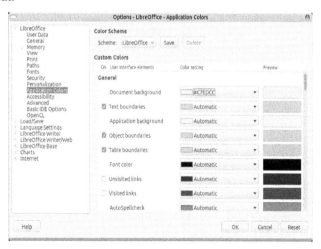

Picture 154: LibreOffice-Aplications Colors window configuration.

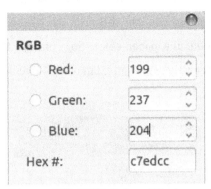

Picture 155: RGB Colour Window

2. Just click the "Document Background Color Setting". And then hit add **custom color.** You will be given new **Pick Color Window** (see Screen-Shot number 3 below). Give these value on to those configuration.

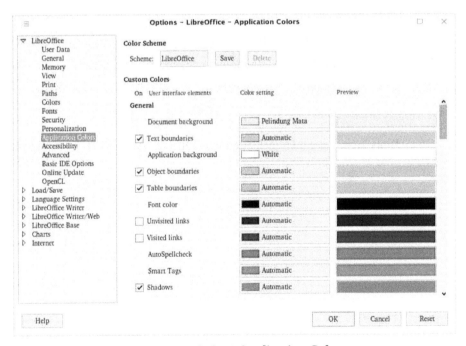

Picture 156: Opsi **Application Colors**

3. Hit OK. Congratulation, you just applied new healthy eye protection paper in LibreOffice.

Bonus: Dracula Theme Configuration for LibreOffice[2]

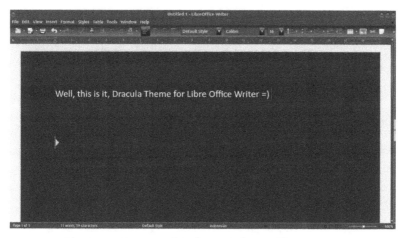

Picture 157: Dracula Theme Libre Office Writer

Recently, i just found GitHub Dracula Theming Project[3] , luckly, in the README.md, the developer published the RGB color value for Dracula theme which is:

Background	Foreground (font color)
40	248
42	248
54	242
#282a36	f8f8f2

Follow the same method as i have mentioned above, to apply this new color theme for your LibreOffice suite.

Credit and Further Reading

The Hex value that i am using in these tutorial is taken from this sites:
http://www.daossoft.com/operating-system-tips/how-to-protect-your-eyes-form-computer-screen.html

The Document Foundation for their countless effort, to bring Free and Open Source Office-Suite

---

2   https://youtu.be/82zki30bQWU for applied Dracula color theme in video format.
3   http://github.com/dracula/dracula-theme

CHAPTER 21

INTRODUCTION TO GRAPHIC

IN LIBREOFFICE WRITER

Copyright © 2016 Azid <paindustry@yahoo.com>

Translated by Risma Fahrul Amin <rismafahrulamin@gmail.com>

When you write a document in LibreOffice Writer, you might want to insert illustration or picture. Applying illustration helps you describing the content, representing visual to the reader, as well as content in magazine or newspaper.

There are 3 type of graphic in LibreOffice Writer:

1. Picture such photo, Scanned picture, or *wallpaper.*
2. Diagram.
3. Graphical Chart.

Manipulating Picture in LibreOffice Writer

LibreOffice Writer has great facility in manipulating Picture, you could import kind of picture format. The most common format are: JPG, PNG, GIF, and BMP. You can rotate, scale, *flip* or *crop* Picture. Besides, you also can edit **SmartArt** from *file* Microsoft Office in LibreOffice Writer.

We can easily manipulate picture in Several usage such transforming picture in black white (*grayscale*). In manipulating Photo or Picture *bitmap*, we can take advantage from **Bitmap Editor** GIMP, while in manipulating **line drawing** (*vector*) we can take **Vector Drawing** Inkscape.

Adding Picture in Writer can be done in several ways such:: *import file, copy-paste* (*clipboard*), *drag and drop* or through *scanner*.

Importing Picture to LibreOffice Writer

1. Firstly, click document to determine location of picture

2. In Menu bar, click **Insert > Image > From File**

3. On *Insert Picture* dialog, you can choose picture which will be imported, then there will be **Preview** and **Link** option. Check **Preview** for displaying chosen Picture and check **Link** if you wan to separate document from picture. Therefore, Picture will not be saved directly onto document which will reduce file capacity. Choose **Keep Link** to create *link* from picture or choose **Embed Graphic** for saving Picture on to document.

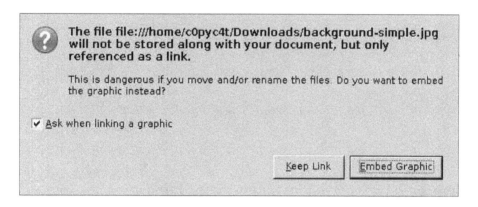

Picture 158: Confirmation window when Link Picture want to be added

Implementation of link in a Picture has advantages and limitations as following explanation:

Advantages:

- Firstly, you can *update* Picture without opening the document as long as *path*/directory and file name has the same as previous picture.

- Second, of course you can also edit picture, and save/*overwrite* your previous picture.

Limitation:

If you want to share a document with your friend, you should give the related picture, and of course you should know folder which the picture was located. This is because the document will not display the picture if the path of the picture was changed or modified.

4. Finally, click **Open** for inserting Picture on to document

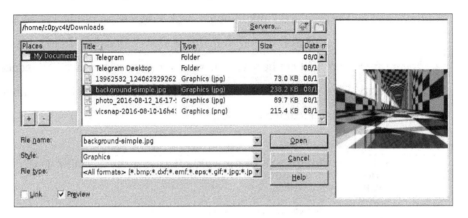

Picture 159: "Insert Picture" Window Dialog

Saving Picture on to Document from *Link*

If you want to save a picture on to document form *link*, you can consider this following explanation:

1. Firstly, click **Edit > Links** in Menu Bar.
2. If you want to *refresh link* of a picture after changing a picture with new one just click **Update.**
3. Click **Break Link.**
4. **Click Yes** for confirmation.
5. Save your document.

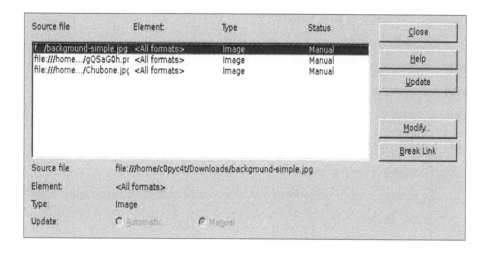

Picture 160: "Edit Links" Window Dialog

Inserting Picture from *Clipboard* or *Copy-Paste*

In LibreOffice Writer, you can do *copy-pasting* picture from other LibreOffice document or application such as GIMP or Inkscape, it is simple to be done, just using **Ctrl + C** on *source* Picture, then **Ctrl + V** on targeted document, or by right clicking to document the choose **Paste**.

In Addition, if source Picture whether other LibreOffice document or other application was *closed* before *paste process is done*, the Picture cant not be pasted.

Inserting Picture from Scanner

If your *scanner* has been connected, LibreOffice Writer could process *scan* command to *scanner* for adding scanned picture on to document. To proceed, pay attention to following steps:

1. Click **Insert** in Menu bar > **Image** > **Scan** > **Select Source** for choosing connected *scanner*.

2. Click **Insert** in Menu bar > **Image** > **Scan** > **Request** to process *scanning picture*.

Adding Picture from Gallery

On Gallery, There are kind of additional image objects such (symbol, icon, *background*, sign, etc) and also sound clip. You can add your own picture to gallery or install *extensions* to add Picture onto Gallery. Follow these steps below in adding picture to Gallery.

1. Click Gallery icon ![icon] on Toolbar, or you can **Tool** in Menu bar > **Gallery**,
2. Then, select the picture.
3. To add the picture onto document, you can *drag n drop* it or right click then choose **Insert**

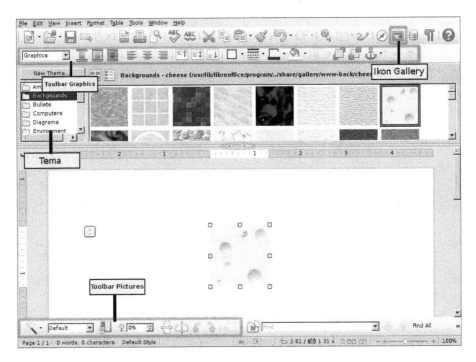

Picture 161: Inserting Picture to document from "Gallery"

Note:

you can *show/hide* Gallery by clicking gallery icon.

Modifying Picture

When you add picture onto document, you might need modify a picture to fit the display into document. In this section, we will explain functionality of: *Toolbar Picture*, *resizing*, *cropping*, and rotate a picture.

In LibreOffice Writer, there are several tools which we can use to modify a picture. But, for professional result, it would be better using separate program such GIMP for *cropping, resize, rotate* or editing color composition from picture then *Insert/Import* it to LibreOffice Writer.

Graphics Mode

To display *toolbar* **Picture**, you can click on the picture or click **View** in Menu bar > **Toolbars** > **Picture**. But, in some circumstance, this menu will not be appeared. This menu will appear as **View** > **Toolbars** > **Image** in newer LibreOffice. Of course, it will have different user interface.

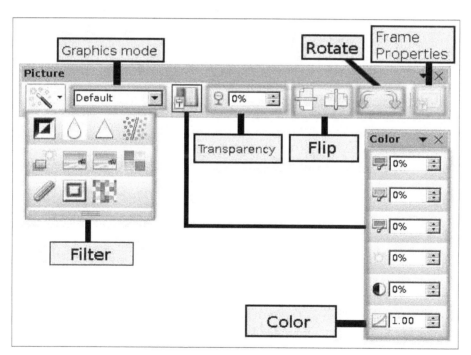

Picture 162: Parts of Toolbar "Picture"

On *Graphics mode* there are *scroll mode* and if it is clicked, there will be a list of options as follow:

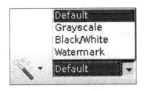

Picture 163: ***Graphics Mode***

Desctiptiom :

Graphics mode	Effect	After Effect
Default	Normal color	
Grayscale	Black and white mode with normal mode	
Black/White	Black and white mode with sharper contrast.	
Watermark	Customizing color in white brightness/bright/transparency mode.	

Flip

To flip Picture vertically or horizontally, click on Picture then click one of icons as follow.

Icon	Flip Mode	Effect
	Flip Vertically	Flip Picture in vertical mode
	Flip Horizontally	Flip Picture in horizontal mode

Table 13: Flip and its function

Filter

These are available Filter on Toolbar Picture with their function/effect:

Icon	Filter Mode	Effect
	Invert	Inverting color to negative effect
	Smooth	Applying *blur* effect on picture
	Sharpen	Increasing contrast to picture
	Remove noise	removing *single-pixels* from Picture
	Solarization	Bright color effect
	Aging	Afternoon effect
	Posterize	Paint color effect

	Pop Art	Applying fade effect
	Charcoal	*Wireframe* effect
	Relief	Applying effect from light angle, shadow, surface protruding effect, then it will be relief effect
	Mosaic	Merge all pixel groups into 1 color area

Table 14: Filter Functions

Note:

Use **Ctrl + Z** or **Alt + Backspace** if you want to undo the effect

Color

Toolbar color can be used to customize RGB component (Red, Green, Blue) on picture, including brightness, contrast and gamma.

Note: if the result of your customization seems unsatisfied, use combined button **Ctrl + Z** to revert your customization

Transparency

This tool is very useful in making watermark effect in a picture. You just need to adjust percentage value on *Transparency* section.

Crop Picture

When you add a picture onto document, you might need eliminate several side parts of a picture. You might just need certain spot from a picture. These following steps will guide you cropping picture in LibreOffice Writer:

1. First, right click on the picture > **Picture** > choose **Crop tab**

2. By default, **Keep Scale option** will be applied, if so, the size of picture after being cropped will be decreased based on cropping size, whereas using **Keep image size**, the cropped area will be as fit as default picture before being cropped. You can also adjust the width and the hieght when using *Keep image size* on *Scale* section.

3. After cropping was applied, click OK to get the result

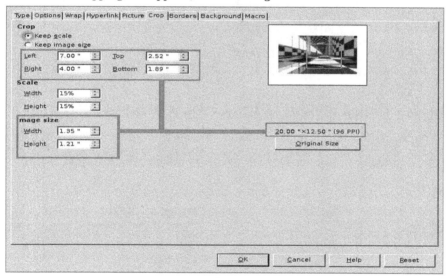

Picture 164: "Keep Scale" Cropping mode

Resize Picture

Resize is easy to be applied, you just need to click on the picture, then drag small green box on one of corners of the picture and pull it until you get appropriate size. By *default*, resize will change just the scale of picture. If you want to adjust the width and the height, press **Shift** while dragging the picture.

Rotating Picture/*Rotate*

To rotate Picture, you can use *Toolbar Picture*

Icon	Name	Effect
↷	Rotate 90 right	Rotating Picture 90 clockwise
↶	Rotate 90 left	Rotating Picture 90 counter clockwise

Table 15: Rotate and its Function

However, LibreOffice Writer provides limited *rotate feature*. You can use LibreOffice Draw or Impress to rotate picture, the copy and paste it to LibreOffice Writer.

Applying *Drawing Tools* in LibreOffice Writer

On *Drawing tools,* there are variation of *shape* (*line, eclipse, rectangle, arrow,* etc). You can use it in making diagram, *charts/flowchart, SmartArt* and *(Fontwork Gallery).*

To show *Drawing Tools* in LibreOffice Writer, click **View** in Menu bar > **Toolbars > Drawing**

Picture 165: "Drawing Tools" bar

The steps in adding *shape* onto document:

1. Click on *shape* which you want to be added.
2. Double click, hold and drag pointer to adjust *shape* size.

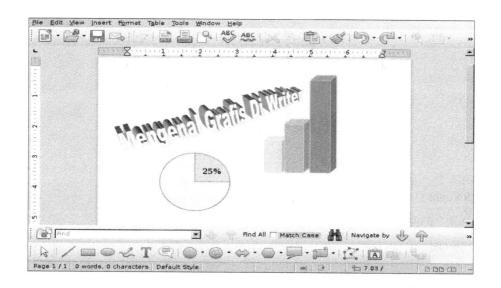

Picture 166: Implementation of *Drawing Tools*

CHAPTER 22

PRINTING ADDRESS LABELS

IN LIBREOFFICE WRITER

Introduction

Label printing is widely used when we want to send a letter of invitation, bills, notices, promotions or other things. If you intend to send invitations then of course data in the form of your name, address, zip code, phone number or others is urgently needed.

Label menu separates as a new menu and does not become one on the mail merge menu, but to activate it later, you still have to access the mail merge menu to bring up the data that has been stored in the database.

The database on this label is the same as the database used for the mail merge. Mail merge is more devoted to use for mail purposes and email header, such as letters or event on the content of the letter itself. As for the labels for the purposes which are not limited to the Affairs of the letter only. You can use it to provide labels on certain devices such as computers, Office inventory of electronic devices, the inventory table Chair or other things.

Still related to database, you can create a specific database for this label using LibreOffice Calc. See example data that I will use for the purpose of printing the label.

	A	B	C	D	E	F	G	H	I	J	K
	motherboard	cpu1	cpu2	memory1	memory2	harddisk	harddisk2	cddrive		powersu	cases	os
	MSI-7641	AMD Athlon II X2 245	2.9 GHz	DDR3 PC3-10700	1 GB	SEAGATE	80 GB	DVDRW LITE-ON, LHAS124	Built-In	Generic	WINDOWS XP
	G41MT-S2PT	Intel Pentium E5700	3.0 GHz	DDR3 PC3-10700	1 GB	Western Digital	160 GB	DVDRW LITE-ON, LHAS124	Built-In	Generic	WINDOWS XP
	ASUS H61M-C	Intel Core i3 3240	3.4 GHz	DDR3 1600	2 GB, TEAM	SEAGATE	160 GB	DVDRW LITE-ON, LHAS124	Built-In	Generic	WINDOWS 7
	BIOSTAR G31M+	Intel Pentium E2180	1.8 GHz		1 GB, LEAM	SEAGATE	80 GB	DVDRW LG, GH22NS70	Built-In	Generic	WINDOWS XP
	JETWAY MIG41T	Intel Pentium E5500	2.8 GHz	DDR3 PC-10600	2 GB, VGEN	SEAGATE	500 GB	DVDRW LG, GH24NS50	Built-In	Generic	WINDOWS XP
	BIOSTAR G31M+	Intel Pentium E2200	2.2 GHz	DDR2 PC-5300	1 GB, VGEN	SEAGATE	80 GB	DVDRW LG, GH24NS50	Built-In	Generic	WINDOWS XP
	ASUS P5GC-MX	Intel Pentium E2180	2.0 GHz	DDR2 PC-6400	1 GB, WRAM	Western Digital	80 GB	SILICON CDROM 52X	Built-In	Generic	WINDOWS XP
	BIOSTAR G31M+	Intel Pentium E2180	1.8 GHz		1 GB, LEAM	SEAGATE	80 GB	DVDRW LG, GH22NS70	Built-In	Generic	WINDOWS XP
	BIOSTAR GF705	Intel Pentium E2200	2.2 GHz	DDR2 PC-5300	512 MB, MEM	SEAGATE	250 GB	DVDRW LG, GH22NS70	Built-In	Generic	WINDOWS XP
	ASUS P5KPL-AM	Intel Pentium E2200	2.2 GHz	DDR2 PC-6400	1 GB, VISIPR	SAMSUNG	80 GB	CDRW SAMSUNG, SH-M52	Built-In	Generic	WINDOWS XP
	ASUS P5G41T-M	Intel Pentium E5700	3.0 GHz	DDR3 PC3-10700	1 GB	SEAGATE	250 GB	DVDRW LG, GH24NS50	Built-In	Generic	WINDOWS XP

Table 16: Data to be Inserted for the creation of a Label

Be sure to follow naming example columns, it means that the data is not needed as a number, a date, or a column of data that will not be used. make sure it is not included.

Ready, Go !

Discussing label is always associated with a paper label that will be used later, and a little tip from me is to make sure to buy it first, and be sure to use the same brand because it is very possible the existence of differences in precision to the same size. And why should I buy it in advance because we have to do a manual setup format margin, spacing each label, length and width of the label.

In the picture below of one of the local label paper that I used to do printing labels.

Picture 167: Picture Label

In the example of the label paper, each page has 9 blank label with each length and width is 5.7 cm and 4 cm. Of course with details which I should size so that the respective information that will be printed on the label could be right on it

Define Database!

To start the labels creation on LibreOffice Writer, select menu New > Labels. The first step is to choose the database that we created earlier (1), the next is to select the data table you want to use (2), if you select the database has many tables of data then customize data tables to be used for mail merge. The next step is to enter the field/column in the selected table (3). From the field/column, we start to set up the data which will be printed on the label. In the picture below I display details Sub Menu on the label. For a review, see box number (5) on the menu.

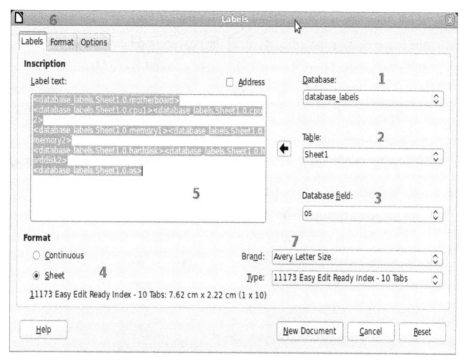

Picture 168: Interface Window Labels on Tab Labels

Paper Layout!

In the previous example, not all existing data in the database is inserted into the label to be printed, bearing the label I would use is not so great. Actually on the menu label itself, there are already some Setup from certain brand label with type that will be used, but due to the brand label is not provided, then at least we should do a Setup for a particular brand and also the type of the brand.

There is some Setup to do any of the following are noteworthy:

1. The number of labels every page, the Setup is represented by stuffing Columns and Row. In the example, the label I would use for number of labels every page is a 9 line settings with 3 columns and 3 rows

2. Margin, is the distance limits of paper up to the labels that will be used. On the setup it just mentioned the distance from the top margin of the paper (Top Margin) as well as the distance from the left margin (Left Margin).

3. *Pitch*, there are two setup. The first is Horizontal Pitch, it is the distance from the edges of the paper (the left) until the next second-label. As for the Vertical Pitch is measured from the top of the paper up to the second label.

4. *Label Size,* The Label Size, it is the size of the label or an empty area which can be used to do printing. Well on the label that I use, they have label with 4 cm and 5.7 cm wide.

5. The width of the paper, and at the moment I am writing this article, the Setup for the paper width on the Page Width and Page Height could not be changed its value corresponds to the length and width of the paper label. the length and width of the paper labels should be 19.3 cm length and 13.8 cm width.

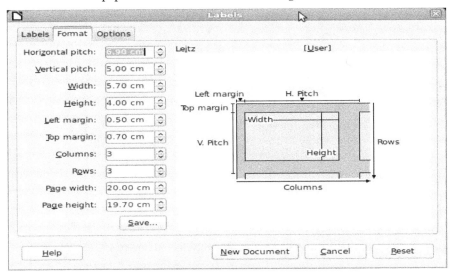

Picture 169: Window Labels interface on the Tab Format

To continue the process, the next is clicking on the **New Document** button, which automatically generates new file. Then there will be 9 data must be enabled via *mail merge.*

Mail Merge

As I have mentioned earlier, to bring up the data on the label we have to access the mail merge menu beforehand. Click the Next button to the entire process up to the final steps of mail merge. When you are prompted to choose whether mail merged documents will be saved or will be directly printed. And here is an illustration of the mail merge process before showing 9 boxes labeled with 3 columns and 3 rows as well as variable data.

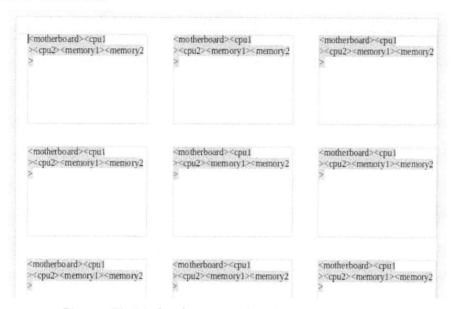

Picture 170: D*isplay the Data in the table Using Mail Merge*

Whereas, in the picture below is the result after the mail merge process.

Picture 171: the end result of the process of making Labels

CHAPTER 23

ARABIC BUCKWALTER CONFIGURATION

IN LIBRE OFFICE WRITER

Copyright © Buono <kangbuono@gmail.com>

Translated by Azis R. Pratama <azis.pratama@gmail.com>

In this tutorial, I'm gonna share my experience using "Arabic Buckwalter" keyboard-layout, to type Arabic letter by using latin-alphabet. For example a = alif, b = ba, and so on.

Step by steps adding new keyboard-layout (in GNU/Linux box):

First of all, we need to adding new keyboard layout into our GNU/Linux system:

1. Open your keyboard preference (it may vary, depends on your current distro & desktop environment). But usually it is accessible via **Start Menu > Setting > Keyboard.** You can also use app launcher like **Albert**, **Gnome-Do** or **Synapse** in order to fire up the keyboard preferences.

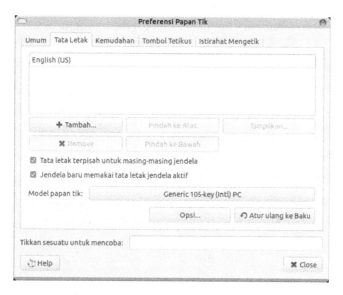

Picture 172: Main Keyboard Control-Panel Preference.

2. In the **keyboard panel preference**, select **Layout TAB (**Tata Letak in Bahasa**)** and then, hit "**Add**" button. You will be given new window configuration (similar to screenshot no. 2 below).

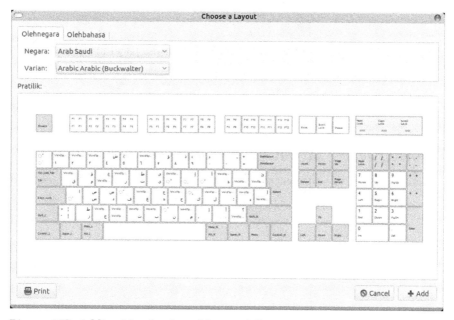

Picture 173: Adding New keyboard-layout (Ubuntu Mate Desktop Environment)

3. Click [Add] button, make sure you select "Arabic (Bukwalter)" keyboard layout and then, hit [OK]. (again, it will be vary, depending on your own distro - desktop environment), but i hope you get the idea how to add and select new keyboard configuration.

Picture 174: New Arabic (Buckwalter) Keyboard Layout.

4. Usually, after you add new keyboard layout, there will be new **"keyboard panel selector"** pop up in your taskbar, here is some examples in the two different desktop environment:

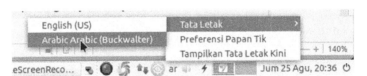

Picture 175: Quickly change keyboard layout using panel in taskbar (Ubuntu Mate)

"Arabic Qwerty" layout Vs. "Arabic Buckwalter" layout

There is some differences between Arabic Qwerty layout and Arabic Buckwalter layout, check this two screenshot below:

Keyboard Arabic Qwerty

Keyboard Arabic Buckwalter

Picture 176: The differences between Arabic **Qwerty** & Arabic **Buckwalter** Keyboard Layout.

Also here is the complete letter conversion from latin to Arabic Buckwalter:

Huruf Latin	Arabic Buckwalter	Huruf Latin	Arabic Buckwalter
a	◌َ	A	ا
s	س	S	ص
d	د	D	ض
f	ف	F	◌ُ
g	غ	G	
h	ه	H	ح
j	ج	J	
k	ك	K	◌ِ
l	ل	L	
;	؛	:	
'	ء	"	
q	ق	Q	

w	و	W	ؤ
Huruf Latin	Arabic Buckwalter	Huruf Latin	Arabic Buckwalter
e		E	ع
r	ر	R	
t	ت	T	ط
y	ي	Y	ى
u	ٌ	U	
i	ٍ	I	إ
o	ٌ	O	أ
p	ة	P	
[		{	آ
]		}	ئ
\		|	آ
z	ز	Z	ظ
x	خ	X	
c		C	
Huruf Latin	Arabic Buckwalter	Huruf Latin	Arabic Buckwalter
v	ث	V	
b	ب	B	
n	ن	N	ْ
m	م	M	
,	،	<	إ
.	ـ	>	أ
/		?	؟

Table 17: Latin to Arabic Buckwalter Table Conversiton

Beginning Typing using Arabic Buckwalter - Keyboard Layout

Before we begin, we need to change the typing method into (right to left). As we know in the Chapter 9 earlier, the keyboard shortcut to change these typing method is: [**Ctrl+Shift+D**] or **Ctrl+Right Shift**. To revert back on to default configuration use [**Ctrl+Shift+A**] or **Ctrl+Left Shift.**

Beside using right to left method, you can also use "**right text alignment**" [CTRL+R] , In order to make our Arabic Buckwalter text displayed correctly.

Picture 177: Right Text Alignment [CTRL+R]

From this point, you can easily typing Arabic Letter, please refer to Table No. 1 above, for a correct Latin to Arabic character translation =)

Picture 178: Arabic Buckwalter in Action

Picture 179: *Right to left, typing method.*

Arabic Buckwalter 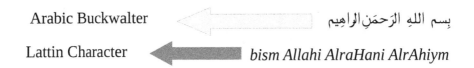 بِسم اللهِ الرَّحمَنِ الرَّاهِيم

Lattin Character *bism Allahi AlraHani AlrAhiym*

Reference:

https://bokunokeiken.wordpress.com/2014/09/24/input-method-arab-dan-jawa-dengan-cara-indonesia/

CHAPTER 24

LIBREOFFICE MOBILITY

Translated by Muhammad Irwan Andriawan <andriawan2014@gmail.com>

LibreOffice Viewer di Android

In the previous chapter, the writer has explained that LibreOffice is one of alternative Free Office softwares from Microsoft Office. It is free to be used, free to be distributed which means you could share LibreOffice installation files to your friends. Along with rapid development of mobile technology, people tend to be lazy creating document in Desktop computer. In certain condition, such in traffic jam where we have deadline to complete tasks, people commonly prefer to use mobile application to create the document.

Nowadays, LibreOffice has landed on Android operating system to support you productivity in term of document creation. Yet, The Document Foundation as LibreOffice maintainer just published a Viewer. As it has been mentioned on LibreOffice manual wiki, You also could port LibreOffice application editor on Android. Unfortunately, LibreOffice editor is still in development state because of several environments and ecosystems on mobile devices itself.

As it has been mentioned on Google Playstore, LibreOffice Viewer has preview feature, whereas for feature of editing document is considered as experimental feature and it is unstable for daily usage. Your feedback and bug report will be considerably required by The Document Foundation as LibreOffice maintainer for quality improvement.

LibreOffice Viewer supports several file format as follows:

- Open Document Format (odt, ods and odp);

- Microsoft Office 2007/2010/2013 (docx, xlsx and pptx);

- Microsoft Office 97/2000 / XP / 2003 (doc, xls and ppt).

LibreOffice Viewer also offers base editing feature such as modifying words in available paragraph and changing font style like bold and italic style. Editing will be improved in the future along with developer community contributions. Users are also invited in reporting problem, seeking bug and attaching related file report on **https://bugs.documentfoundation.org**.

LibreOffice Viewer utilize the same basic program as LibreOffice for Microsoft Windows, Apple Mac OS X and GNU/Linux. It is also combined with new front end (Interface and appearance) based on Firefox application for Android, so that reading document on Android will be familiar with LibreOffice in desktop mode. LibreOffice was released under Mozilla Public License v2.

The Contributors

LibreOffice Viewer is developed by collabora dan Igalia, supported by Smoose, with contribution from student who participate in *Google Summer of Code* in collaboration with The Document Foundation and LibreOffice society. SUSE has given the main foundation in supporting cross platform compatibility and several core component from Mozilla Corporation. Thousand appreciation for independent LibreOffice contributor who has contributed code since 2010.

You could fully contribute as contributor by visiting **http://www.libreoffice.org/about-us/credits**. besides, you could download LibreOffice Viewer on **https://play.google.com/store/apps/details?id=org.documentfoundation.libreoffice**.

Interface of LibreOffice Viewer on Android

Picture 180: LibreOffice Viewer Appearance when Opening Text Document on Android

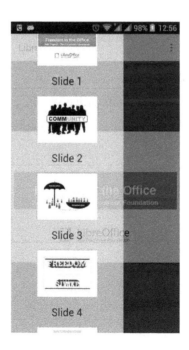

Picture 181: LibreOffice Viewer Appearance when Opening Presentation Document on Android

CHAPTER 25

INSERTING MATH FORMULA ON

LIBREOFFICE WRITER

We often found Math Formula in various document, like textbook till essay / thesis. It recently requires us to understand about how to using Math formula or Math equations correctly.

On LibreOffice, To process math equations is already provided separately from LibreOffice Writer, specifically Math. However we still can insert math equations to Writer.

Inserting Math Formula

To insert Math Equations to LibreOffice Writer, we can access menu **Insert** > **Object** > **Formula**. Then Writer will display like figure below.

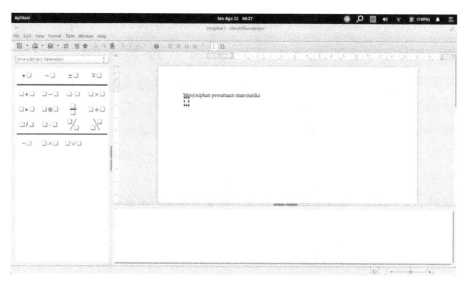

Picture 182: Interface of LibreOffice Math

At the figure above, we can find three main workspaces of LibreOffice Math. In the top section, there is **Results Window.** The bottom section is **Command Window** where a place for Math Syntax, and The left side is **Elements**, a set of math symbols and math operators which already grouped by category.

Then, to Insert Math Formula. There is three methods which is usual to use, such as click & edit syntax and directly type math formula (on math interface or outside math interface)

Method Click and Edit Syntax (on Math Interface)

For Example, we want to insert formula $y = \frac{3x^2}{5}$, then the steps is as follows :

1. At **Command Window**, type **y =**

2. Click Category **Unary/Binary Operators** at **Elements** panel, then click

3. At Result Window, click twice in the upper box. A place for $3x^2$

4. Type 3, then choose **Functions** category at **Elements** panel. Click icon $\square^{\square}$.

5. At Result Window, click twice where a place for **x**, then type *x*.

6. Next click twice where a place for **power 2**, then type **2**.

7. Next click twice in the lower box. A place for **5**, then type **5**.

8. After finish all above. Click outside the formula box.

At this method, we can also press keyboard shortcut F4 to move from either box to another box.

Directly Typing Method (on Math Interface)

This method is the most effective method, to make some math formulas. Then we just type math notation on **Command Window**. For example, if we want to insert math equation $y=\dfrac{3x^2}{5}$, then we just type: **y={3x^2} over 5** then press **Esc**.

Directly Typing Method (Outside of Math Interface)

We also need to know, this directly type method can also be done outside of Math Interface. It means that we don't need to enter Math Interface before we type some formulas. This method can be done as follows :

1. Type Math formula which we want insert to the document, for example **y={3x^2}over5**.

2. Block selected Math formula.

3. Access menu **Insert > Object > Formula**.

Automatically, the mentioned Math formula we type before will change to math equation $y=\dfrac{3x^2}{5}$.

From three methods to insert Math formula and Math equations, the last method is the most favorite writer methods. And surely, to easily use this directly type method, we need to understand some syntax which explain on next sub chapter.

By default, every time we edit / change math syntax on **Command Window**. The results on **Results Window** will automatically updated. If a result not automatically updated on **Results Window**, we can press **F9** or access menu **View > Update,** or we can surely **View > AutoUpdate Display** already checked / activated.

Various Math Formula on LibreOffice Math

To insert Math formula or Math Syntax, there is some syntaxs we need to understand like basic operators (Addition, Subtraction, Multiplication and Division), Fractions, Powers, Roots, Symbols and Matrix. Read more on some table below.

Basic Operators

Symbol for basic math operators can be found on **Unary/Binary Operators** category.

Result	Syntax	Result	Syntax
$a+b$	a + b	$x>y$	x > y
$a-b$	a - b	$x\geq y$	x >= y
$a\times b$	a times b	$x<y$	x < y
$a\div b$	a div b	$x\leq y$	x <= y
$x\pm 4$	x +-4	$x\neq y$	x <> y

Table 18: Result and Syntax of Math Basic Operations

Fractions

Symbol for fractions can be found on Unary/Binary Operators category.

Result	Syntax	Result	Syntax
$\frac{a}{b}$	a over b		
a/b	a slash b	a/b	a wideslash b
$a\backslash b$	a bslash b	$\backslash\frac{b}{a}$	a widebslash b

Table 19: Result and Syntax of Fractions

With the following syntax above, we can make Math formulas as follows:

Result	Syntax
$y=\dfrac{a+b}{c}$	y = {a+b} over c
$x=1+\dfrac{1}{2+\dfrac{3}{5}}$	x = 1+ {1 over {2+{3 over 5}}}

Result	Syntax
$y=\dfrac{\dfrac{a}{b}+c}{d}$	y = {{a over b}+c} over d

Table 20: Example of fraction results

Roots

Symbol for roots can be found on Functions category.

Result	Syntax
$\sqrt{n}$	sqrt {n}
$\sqrt[n]{m}$	nroot {n} {m}

Table 21: Result and Syntax of Roots

With the following syntax above, we can make Math formulas as follows:

Result	Syntax
$y=\sqrt{\dfrac{a}{b+c}}$	y = sqrt{a over{b+c}}
$y=\sqrt[5]{\dfrac{a}{b+c}}$	y = nroot{5}{a over{b+c}}

Table 22: Example of Roots results

Powers and Index

Symbol for Powers can be found on **Functions** category.

Result	Syntax
x^n	x^n
y_n	y_n
e^n	func e^{n}

Result	Syntax
$\exp(n)$	exp(n)

Table 23: Result and Syntax of Powers and Index

With the following syntax above, we can make Math formulas as follows:

Result	Syntax
$x_{1.2}=\dfrac{-b\pm\sqrt{b^2-4\,ac}}{2\,a}$	x_{1.2} = {-b +-sqrt{b^2 – 4ac}} over {2a}
$x=\sqrt{2}^{\sqrt{2}^{\sqrt{2}}}$	x = {sqrt2}^{{sqrt2}^{ {sqrt2}^... }}
$C_0^n=1$	C^{n}_{0} = 1
$f(x)=e^{2x-3}$	f(x)=func e^{2x-3}

Table 24: Example Powers and Index results

Brackets

Brackets can be found on Brackets category.

Result	Syntax
n	{n}
(n)	(n)
$[n]$	[n]
$[\![n]\!]$	ldbracket n rdbracket
$\{n\}$	lbrace n rbrace
$\langle n\rangle$	langle n rangle
$\langle m\vert n\rangle$	langle m mline n rangle
$\lceil n\rceil$	lceil n rceil
$\lfloor n\rfloor$	lfloor n rfloor
$\vert n\vert$	lfloor n rfloor
$\Vert n\Vert$	ldline n rdline

Table 25: Result and Syntax of Brackets

At table above, we can understand that sign "{" and "}" can't directly generate brackets sign.

However, to type brackets like table above can't adjust / fit height of notation which flanked. Therefore we need to add "left" before left bracket and "right" before right bracket. Refer to the following example!

Result	Syntax
$y = \left(1 + \dfrac{a}{b}\right)^2$	y = (1+a over b)^2
$y = \left(1 + \dfrac{a}{b}\right)^2$	y = left (1+a over b right)^2

Table 26: Comparison of usual brackets and adjusting brackets

If we want to displays only one brackets, we can implement few method as follows!

Result	Syntax
$f(x) = \langle \dfrac{ax}{b}$	f(x)= \langle {ax} over {b}
$f(x) = \begin{cases} ax+b \\ 0 \\ -x \end{cases}$	f(x) = left lbrace { stack{""ax+b # ""0 # ""-x }}right none

Table 27: displaying one brackets

Limit, Sum, Product, and Integral

Typing sigma notation, limit, or integral can be found on **Operator** category.

Result	Syntax
$\lim\limits_{x \to a} f(x)$	lim from {x toward a} f(x)
$\sum\limits_{x=k}^{n} U_k$	sum from {x = k} to{n} U_k
$\prod\limits_{x=k}^{n} U_k$	prod from {x = k} to{n} U_k
$\int f(x)\, dx$	int f(x) dx

Result	Syntax
$\int_a^b f(x)\,dx$	int from a to b f(x) dx

Table 28: Result and Syntax of Limit operators, Sum, Product and Integral

With the following syntax above, we can make Math formulas as follows:

Result	Syntax
$\lim\limits_{x\to\frac{4}{3}}\dfrac{6x^2+7x-20}{\sqrt{9x^2-24x+16}}$	lim from{x toward {4 over 3}}{ { 6x^2+7x-20 } over { sqrt{9x^2-24x+16} }}
$\sum\limits_{k=0}^{\infty}\dfrac{1}{1+k+k!}$	sum from {k=0} to {infinity} {1 over {1+k+fact{k}}}
$\int_0^{\infty}\dfrac{\sin(x)}{x}\,dx=\dfrac{\pi}{2}$	int from 0 to infinity {{sin(x)} over x dx} = %pi over 2

Table 29: Example Limit Operators, Sum, dan Integral

Trigonometry

Typing trigonometry notation can be found on **Functions** category.

Result	Syntax	Result	Syntax
$\sin(x)$	sin(x)	y	"cosec"(x)
$\cos(x)$	cos(x)	$\sec(x)$	"sec"(x)
$\tan(x)$	tan(x)	$\cot(x)$	cot(x)

Table 30: Result and Syntax of Trigonometry functions

With the following syntax above, we can make Math formulas as follows:

Result	Syntax
$\sin\left(\dfrac{2\pi-5}{8}\right)$	sin left({2%pi-5}over{8}right)
$\dfrac{\tan(x+\sqrt{3})}{1+\tan(x-\sqrt{3})}$	{tan (x+sqrt{3})} over {1 + tan(x - sqrt{3})}

Table 31: Example Trigonometry functions

Logarithm

Typing logarithm notation can be found on **Functions** category.

Result	Syntax	Result	Syntax
$\log(x)$	log (x)	$\log_b(n)$	log_b (n)
$\ln(x)$	ln (x)	$^b\log(n)$	{log (n)} lsup b

Table 32: Result and Syntax of Logarithm functions

With the following syntax above, we can make Math formulas as follows:

Result	Syntax
$^a\log(b)\cdot{}^b\log(c)={}^a\log(c)$	{log (b)} lsup a cdot {log (c)} lsup b = {log (c)} lsup a
$f(t)=\dfrac{\ln(t)-1}{t}$	f(t) = {ln(t)-1} over {t}

Table 33: Example Logarithm functions

Matrix

Inserting matrix, can be found on **Formats** category. However, only limited for 2×2 matrix size. for more than that, Refer to the following example !

Result	Syntax
$\begin{matrix} a & b \\ c & d \end{matrix}$	matrix{ a # b ## c # d }
$\begin{matrix} a & b & c \\ d & e & f \end{matrix}$	matrix{ a # b # c ## d # e # f }
$\begin{matrix} a & b \\ c & d \\ e & f \end{matrix}$	matrix{ a # b ## c # d ## e # f }
$\begin{pmatrix} a & b \\ c & d \end{pmatrix}$	left (matrix{ a # b ## c # d } right)

$\begin{vmatrix} a & b \\ c & d \end{vmatrix}$	left lline matrix{ a # b ## c # d } right rline

Table 34: Result and Syntax of Matrix

Make sure that each column separated by one hash tag (#) and each row separated by two hash tag (##). Then, we can make more than 2×2 matrix size.

Result	Syntax
$A^{-1}=\dfrac{1}{\begin{vmatrix} a & b \\ c & d \end{vmatrix}}\times\begin{pmatrix} d & -b \\ -c & a \end{pmatrix}$	A^{-1}={1}over{size*0.6 left lline matrix{ a # b ## c # d } right rline} times left (matrix{ d # -b ## -c # a } right)

Table 35: Example Matrix equation

Symbols

There are two methods to insert symbol, specifically access menu **Tools > Symbols** and directly type some symbols. If we use first method, then will display dialog box as follows :

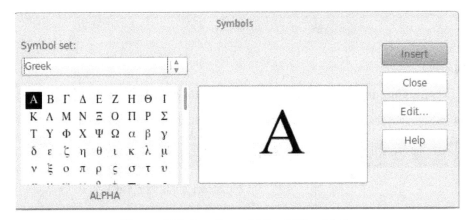

Picture 183: Interface of LibreOffice Math

On **Symbol Set**, we can choose **Greek** symbol for Greece symbols, **iGreek** for Greece symbols italic version, and **Special** for special symbols. Choose symbols which you want insert, then click **Insert**. Last click **Close**, to close **Symbols** dialog box.

And the second method, we can directly type the name of the following symbols through dialog box. Begins with "%" sign. For example, typing *%alpha* will result α symbol.

More for symbol syntax can be found in the following table :

Symbol	Syntax	Symbol	Syntax
α	%alpha	A	%ALPHA
β	%beta	B	%BETA
γ	%gamma	Γ	%GAMMA
δ	%delta	Δ	%DELTA
ε	%epsilon	E	%EPSILON
ζ	%zeta	Z	%ZETA
η	%eta	H	%ETA
θ	%theta	Θ	%THETA
ι	%iota	I	%IOTA
κ	%kappa	K	%KAPPA
λ	%lambda	Λ	%LAMBDA
μ	%mu	M	%MU
ν	%nu	N	%NU
ξ	%xi	Ξ	%XI
ο	%omicron	O	%OMICRON
π	%pi	Π	%PI
ρ	%rho	P	%RHO
σ	%sigma	Σ	%SIGMA
τ	%tau	T	%TAU
υ	%upsilon	Y	%UPSILON
φ	%phi	Φ	%PHI
χ	%chi	X	%CHI
ψ	%psi	Ψ	%PSI
ω	%omega	Ω	%OMEGA
ϑ	%vartheta	ϖ	%varpi
ϱ	%varrho	ς	%varsigma

Table 36: Result and Syntax for Greece symbols

for symbols on **iGreek** subsets, yo just adding "i" in the beginning of symbol name. For example, "*%itheta*" for producing θ .

for **Specials** subset you can use following table syntax:

Special	Syntax	Special	Syntax
‰	%perthousand	→	%tendto
∈	%element	∉	%noelement
≡	%identical	≠	%notequal
∧	%and	∨	%or
∡	%angle	∡	%Ux2221

Table 37: Result and Syntax for some special characters

Inserting New Rows, Space, and Formula

In Writing Formula, maybe we realize the distance of some characters is too tight. However with directly pressing *space* on *keyboard* will not affect space on formula. Therefore we can using **{}** , ` , ~ , or **"<space>"** (space which flanked with quotes) to give space on formula. For complete example you can use following table syntax:

Result	Syntax	Information
$a+b$	a+b	Using Space won't
$a+b$	a + b	affect Formula
$a+b$	a{}+b	Give little space
$a+b$	a`+b	before "+" sign
$a+b$	a~+b	Give one space
$a+b$	a" "+b	before "+" sign

Table 38: Few example methods to give space on Math Formula

Sometimes typing Math Formula we need more than one row. As well as using **Space**, pressing **Enter** on **Command Window** never generate new line / row on the following Math formula. To do that, we using "newline" syntax to start new line.

Result	Syntax
$y=2x+5+3$ $y=2x+8$	y=2x+5+3 newline y=2x+8

Table 39: Generating new line on Math Formula

When we notice it, the result of math Formula will automatically arranged to center alignment. That will look not fit if we use for typing solution of Math equation. Therefore we can set alignment using alignl to align left and alignr to align right. For complete example you can use following table syntax:

Result	Syntax
$y=2x+5+3$ $y=2x+8$	alignl y=2x+5+3 newline alignl y=2x+8
$y=2x+5+3$ $y=2x+8$	alignr y=2x+5+3 newline alignr y=2x+8

Table 40: Set Left Align and Right Align on Math Formula

Typing more complex solution, using newline and spacing will make syntax has already written seems very complicated. Therefore we can combine with matrix. For complete example you can use following table syntax:

Result	Syntax
$\begin{aligned} y - y_1 &= m(x - x_1) \\ y - 5 &= 2(x - 3) \\ y - 5 &= 2x - 6 \\ y &= 2x - 6 + 5 \\ y &= 2x - 1 \end{aligned}$	matrix{ alignr y-y_1 #"="# alignl m(x-x_1) ## alignr y-5 #"="# alignl 2(x-3) ## alignr y-5 #"="# alignl 2x-6 ## alignr y #"="# alignl 2x-6+5 ## alignr y #"="# alignl 2x-1 }

Table 41: example of writing solution (*step-by-step*)

Inserting certain attributes

Sometimes formula we already typed give lacking / not satisfy result or not accord with our expectations. With **Attribute** category we can set result, whether size, type, font color and another expected attribute.

Result	Syntax	Keterangan
$2 + \mathbf{3} = 5$	2+bold{3}=5	Bold number 3
$2 + \mathit{3} = 5$	2+italic{3}=5	Italic number 3
$\underline{2+3} = 5$	underline{2+3}=5	Add Underline on 2+3
$\overline{AB} + \overline{BC} = \overline{AC}$	overline{AB} +overline{BC}=overline{AC}	Add Overline (Upper line) on AB, BC, dan AC
$\sin\frac{\pi}{4} = \cos\frac{\pi}{4}$	font sans {sin{%pi over 4}}= font serif {cos {%pi over4}}	Change font $\sin\frac{\pi}{4}$ become Sans, and on $\cos\frac{\pi}{4}$ become Serif.
$\log(x) = 1$	color red {log(x)}=1	Give red color on $\log(x)$
x	size 18 x	Change font size to 18 pt

Table 42: Giving some additional Attributes on Math Formula

By using Attribute, we can improve Math formula result which sometimes lacking. Especially when typing fragments. Look at example below !

Result	Syntax
$x_{1.2}=\dfrac{-b\pm\sqrt{b^2-4ac}}{2a}$	x_{1.2} = {{-b +-sqrt{b^2 − 4ac}} over {2a}}
$x_{1.2}=\frac{-b\pm\sqrt{b^2-4ac}}{2a}$	Size 8 {x_{1.2} = {{-b +-sqrt{b^2 − 4ac}} over {2a}} }
$x_{1.2}=-b\pm\frac{\sqrt{b^2-4ac}}{2a}$	size*0.7{x_{1.2} = {{-b +-sqrt{b^2 − 4ac}} over {2a}} }
$x_{1.2}=-b\pm\frac{\sqrt{b^2-4ac}}{2a}$	size-5{x_{1.2} = {{-b +-sqrt{b^2 − 4ac}} over {2a}} }
$x_{1.2}=\frac{-b\pm\sqrt{b^2-4ac}}{2a}$	x_{1.2}=size*0.6{{{-b+-sqrt{b^2-4ac}}over{2a}}}

Table 43: Example to adjust font size on Math formula

Note that we can adjust font size on formula very easily and very dynamic.

- At the first row, by default font size on formula is 12pt
- At the second row, we set font size become 8pt using **size 8** command.
- At the third row, we change font size become 70% of default font size, (12pt*70%=8.4pt) using **size*0.7** command.
- At the fourth row, we reduce font 5 point from default font size (12pt-5pt = 7pt) using **size -5** command.
- At the fifth row, font size on $x_{1.2}=$ using defaut font size, and $\frac{-b\pm\sqrt{b^2-4ac}}{2a}$ we reduce to 60% default size.

Discovering another Syntax Math Formula

From few examples above, actually there are still some notations which not explained in here. All of following notations can be accessed through **Elements**. Through **Elements**, we can also discover existing syntax.

For example we will write absolute equation $|2x-9|\geq0$. Then we choose **Functions** category and ▢ icon. It will give result on **Command Window** that those symbols for "absolute value" have "abs" syntax on **Command Window.**

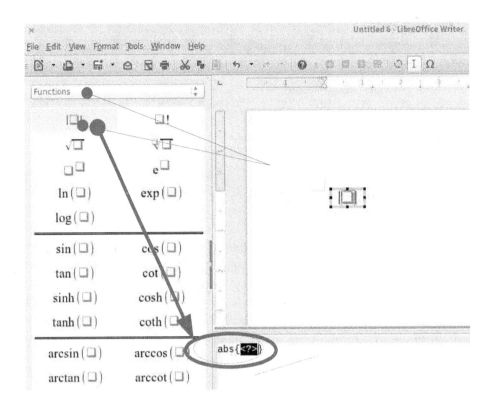

Picture 184: Discovering Syntax of Math Formula

CHAPTER 26
PRINTING DOCUMENTS
ON LIBREOFFICE WRITER

Translated by <ari>

After a document is created and finished, the last step you might want to do is to print it. On LibreOffice, documents we have created can be printed as PDF files or we can print them on papers.

Printing documents as PDF files was explained on chapter 14. Sometime, we want to keep LibreOffice documents as PDF when we want to print them on other computers that might not have LibreOffice installed, like at print shops. So we can keep our documents formatting that might be changed by other Word Processor applications if we saved them on an editable format.

PDF format is also used as soft copy on documents exchanges. For example, Indonesian Government's Ministry of Communication and Information in its 2013 regulation requires all of the official documents must be either on open document format (odf) or as portable data format (pdf).

Steps on Printing Documents

Before printing a document on papers, make sure the document is already final, you can see how will it looks on paper from *print preview*. From menu **File > Print Preview** or click ⏴ 🖶 🔍 shortcut on toolbar.

You can see document *print preview* in this image:

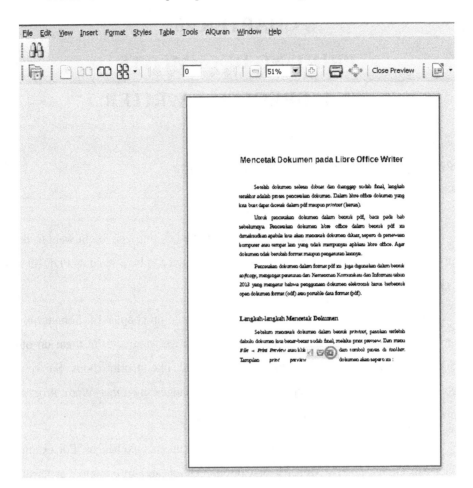

Picture 185: Example of Print Preview

Printer *Settings*

1. You can access printer settings from **Start Menu > Setting > Printer** or from search menu, type "*printer*" (without quotes).

2. Then double click the printer you want to use. Set *printer* as your usual work requires.

*Note: For printing in **F4** size, you can use **legal** size instead. It is possible to add settings to **/etc/cups/ppd/** but it does not always works and may produce errors.*

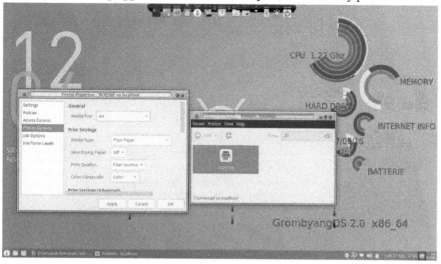

Picture 186: Printer Properties windows

Printing Documents

1. You can print documents from **File > Print.** By using **Ctrl + P** keyboard shortcut or by clicking this icon on toolbar.

2. You will be presented with this window:

Picture 187: Print window

3. The next step is to set Properties according the type and orientation of the paper you use.

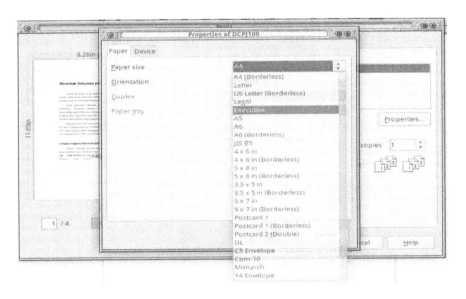

Picture 188: Printer Properties window

4. Then click **OK** and **Print**.

Adding F4 Paper on Printer Settings

I (writer) have never manually added extra settings to print documents on **F4** paper. By selecting **legal** in place of **F4** size I have never encountered any problem when printing from LibreOffice Writer, LibreOffice Calc, or LibreOffice Impress. Adding manually paper size is not recommended because its risk introducing some problems.

But, if you want to try it yourself, here is the steps:

1. On command line, enter **cd /etc/cups/ppd/** to move to printer settings files directory. Inside you will find configuration files for your printers. In this example the file is *DCPJ100.ppd*. You should adjust accordingly.

Picture 189: The view of Nautilus /etc/cups/ppd/

2. Backup the original files, so you can restore them if necessary. From command line :

cp /etc/cups/ppd/DCPJ100.ppd /etc/cups/ppd/DCPJ100.ppd.bak

3. Edit the ppd file, we are using Gedit text editor here.

    sudo gedit DCPJ100.ppd

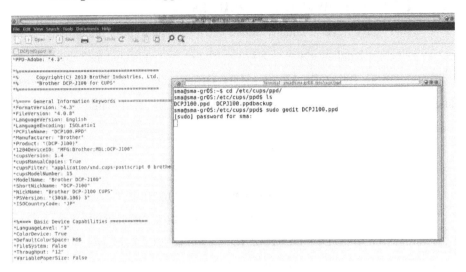

Picture 190: Ppd file in Gedit text editor.

4. In Gedit, press **CTRL+H** to open Replace dialog window. Type *1008* in
    Search for box and type *936* in ***Replace with*** box. **Save** and then **Close**.

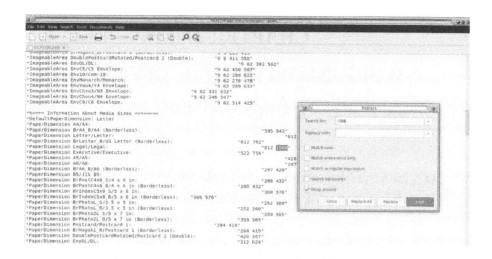

Picture 191: Find and Replace window on Gedit

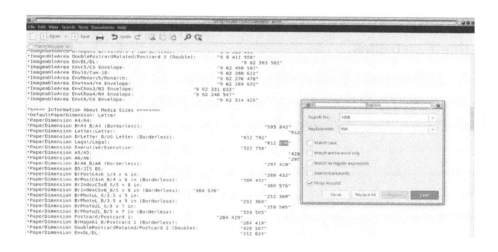

Picture 192: Gedit view after the values are replaced

5. Restart running **CUPS** service by typing in command line **sudo /etc/init.d/cups restart**

6. Done. Before using the new setting, you need to close all of active LibreOffice instances. You can now select the size **Legal** when you print on **F4** paper.

CHAPTER 27

WORKING WITH LIBREOFFICE

EXTENSION

Translated by Muhammad Irwan Andriawan <andriawan2014@gmail.com>

Extension is an add-on tools which can separately install or uninstall from LibreOffice main program. *Extension* could create new formulas or functions which improve existing functionality of functions.

Getting Extensions

To obtain LibreOffice *Extension*, We could access following link http://extensions.libreoffice.org/extension-center. There are various *extensions* for all LibreOffice components, include LibreOffice Writer.

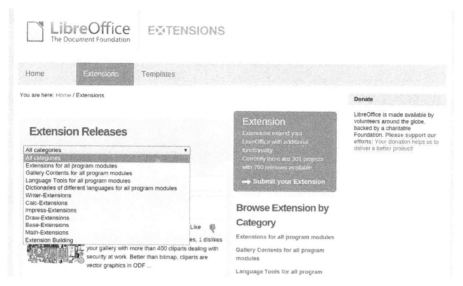

Picture 193: Choosing Extension by certain category

Downloaded *Extension* has ".oxt" file format. This Extension is ready to install on LibreOffice.

Installing *Extension*

To install and activate *Extension*, double click the *extension* which would be installed to. There will be a *pop up* window contains installation confirmation of Extension as following illustration:

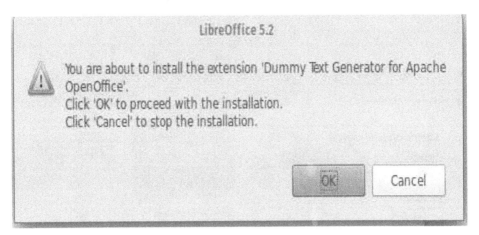

Picture 194: Installation confirmation of Extension

Click OK button to continue to **Extension Software License Agreement** window. In this occasion, we would be asked to read License Agreement from the *Extension*. Navigate to the last section or click **Scroll Down button** to read whole License. **Accept button** would be activated, just click **Accept button**.

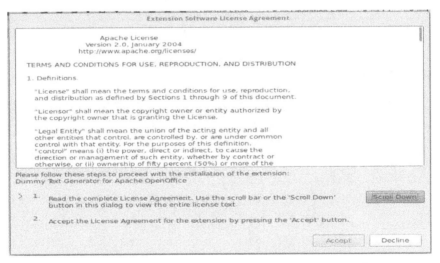

Picture 195: Extension Software License Agreement window

Take a couple of time, until installation process is done as following illustration.

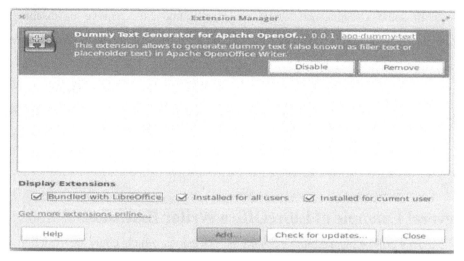

Picture 196: *Extension Manager* Window

we could add other *extensions* by clicking **Add... button** then choose other *extension* which we would be installed. Click **Close button** for closing Extension Manager window, then re-run LibreOffice Writer. The Installed E*xtension* is ready to be used.

Managing Extension

To find out what Extension is enabled on LibreOffice Writer, we could check it on **Extension Manager window** as previous illustration above. To open Extension Manager window, we could navigate to menu bar **Tools > Extension** or use *shortcut keyboard* **Ctrl+Alt+E**. Make sure "Bundled with LibreOffice", "Installed for all user", and "Installed for current user" on **Display Extensions** are checked for displaying all installed extensions.

When we choose one of available extension, there are 2 available options, they are **Disable** and **Remove**. If we choose Disable, selected *Extension* would be disabled, without uninstall it. To enable selected Extension click **Enable button**. If we choose *Remove* option, The selected *Extension* would be disabled then remove it from Extension list. We need to re-install to activate removed extension.

In some circumstance, while we install, uninstall, remove or disable an extension, there would be unexpected condition such freezing extension state, or even crash state which caused LibreOffice issues force close. These occasion due to an extension is made by third party which potentially could not cover compatibility issue from The extension itself. Thus, we strongly recommend saving all opened documents before managing extension.

Several Example of LibreOffice Writer *Extension*

This following example of various extensions which could be installed on LibreOffice writer. Several extensions might be not working as we are expected.

Clipart Gallery of Danger Signs

This e*xtension* contains collection of clipart danger *signs*. After installing this *extension*, we could view it through **Insert > Media > Gallery** or through right-side panel, choose **Sidebar setting icon > Gallery**. You could download it on **http://extensions.libreoffice.org/extension-center/gallery-of-danger-signs**.

Picture 197: Collections of Clipart Danger Signs

TexMath

If we often work with LaTeX and want to insert mathematical notation such LaTex-based document, this *extension* is very powerful for alternative solution. To enable this *extension*, we have to install texlive first.

After Installing this extension successfully, this extension icon would appear

which contains interface for inserting mathematical notation, configuring TexMaths, and recompiling existing mathematical notation.

We just need to click the *icon* π then it would appear input formula window. Type formula which we want to insert then click **LaTeX**. Similar to LibreOffice Math, we also could directly type mathematical notation on LibreOffice Writer by blocking selected formula, then click Icon π .

You could download TexMath extension on website **http://extensions.libreoffice.org/extension-center/texmaths-1**.

Dummy Text Generator

If we delight to create template, we might be familiar with *dummy text* such as Lorem ipsum. With this *extension*, we could easily generate *dummy text* through **Insert > Dummy Text**. But, for generating Lorem ipsum template, we need Internet connection.

You could download Dummy Text Creator extension on https://www.arielch.org/aoo/aoo-dummy-text/ .

Dmath

This extension is very helpful in Drawing mathematical objects such as, angle, triangle, Nominal line, Cartesian coordinates, etc. After installing this extension, there will be a new menu Dmath and toolbar icon which contains kind of mathematical object feature.

You could download Dummy Dmath extension on **http://extensions.libreoffice.org/extension-center/dmaths**.

Writer Rotation Tool

This *extension* is a-must extension on LibreOffice Writer. Through this extension, we could rotate picture which we have inserted on to LibreOffice directly with mouse.

To rotate desired picture, click selected picture, then click icon **on toolbar, the picture would be rotated by mouse.** You could download **Writer Rotation Tool** on **http://extensions.libreoffice.org/extension-center/writerrotationtool**.

CHAPTER 28

WORKING WITH TRACK CHANGES

Translated by Muhammad Irwan Andriawan <andriawan2014@gmail.com>

Track Changes

Track changes is a subheading menu in LibreOffice writer. You can easily find it on Edit Menu Bar. There is slight different naming menu in LibreOffice writer under version 4 especially in Edit menu. In Earlier version 4, Track changes appears as Changes in Edit menu. But, in the latest version 5, it uses Track changes. both has identical usage.

Literally, track changes has meaning jejak perubahan in Bahasa. Track changes has great functionality in:

1. Recording changes in a document

2. Making collaborative editing easier

Recording changes in a document

Track changes feature is not activated yet by default. To activate it, navigate to menu bar **Edit > Track Changes/ Changes > Record Changes**. If you want to make it simple, Just use shortcut key combination **Ctrl + Shift + E**.

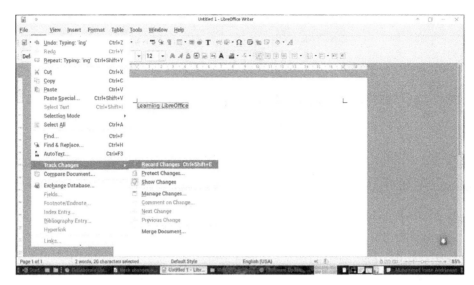

Picture 198: Track Changes Feature

After track changes was enabled, Document will have special record history. It can be identify from underlined phrase in Illustration below.

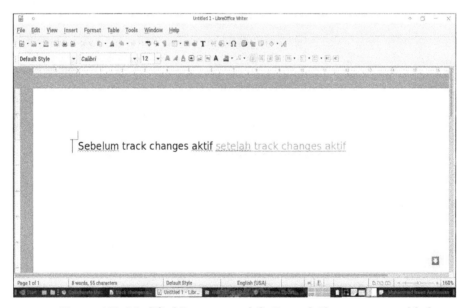

Picture 199: Modified Document while *Record Changes* was enabled

In certain circumstance, we could not see special mark underlined and golden font effect. It is because we do not enable **show changes feature** yet. Navigate to menu **Edit > Track Changes/Changes > Show changes** if you want to activate it.

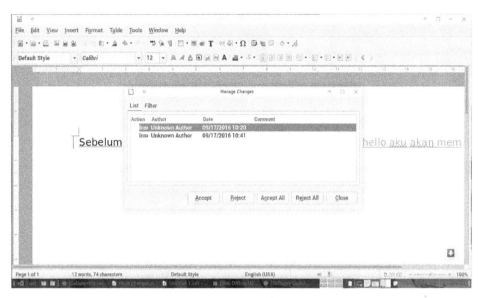

Picture 200: Manage Changes Window

Simply said, *track changes* records everything changes you have been made. It could be font color usage, font style, size and content of document itself. But, in advanced usage, track changes can help us organizing document in well manner. We can track changes in **Manage Changes Feature**.

You can access *Manages Changes* in menu **Edit > Track Changes/Changes > Manages changes.** *Manage Changes* will appear serving you detail information about all changes in two tab menu **List** and **Filter**. In tab menu *List*, you can find **Action, Author, Date** and **Comment**.

1	*Action*	What changes which we has been made
2	*Insertion*	Changes which related to insertion
3	*Deletion*	Changes which related to deletion
4	*Author*	Identity of Changes editor
5	*Date*	Changes date
6	*Comment*	Additional Information related to changes

In tab **Filter**, you could do filtering information related to changes

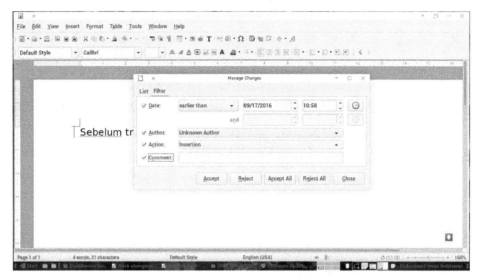

Picture 201: Tab Menu Filter

besides tab menu, there are 5 common *button in Manage Changes*, they are **Accept, Reject, Accept All, Reject All,** and **Close**.

1	*Accept*	Accept certain changes to be part of document. When someone else try to make a changes, all his change will be recorded in the list. You as an owner of the document could accept it as a part of document
2	*Reject*	In contrary with *accept button, reject button* deny changes made in document. When you decide to reject certain changes, the document will clear the changes from list and also from content of document itself.
3	*Accept All*	This button has the same functionality with *accept button*, but it will accept all changes record in the list.
4	*Reject All*	This button has the same functionality with *reject button*, but it will deny all changes record in the list.
5	*Close*	Close *Manage Changes* window

Making collaborative editing easier

Advanced implementation of *track changes/changes feature* could be the best alternative in collaborative document editing. This term will match following circumstance:

- You are an editor or writer who conducting collaborative project and your team spread out in different location.

- You are a graduate student who are in Thesis writing project. You have high scheduled Lecturer as your thesis supervisor

Through *track changes feature* collaborative editing and writing could possibly be done. In addition, all the feature will make people easily tracking changes in document. It surely makes editing and writing in LibreOffice writer more productive.

CHAPTER 29

MAKING CHART

IN LIBREOFFICE WRITER

Chart is 2D graphical object which represent value or result in bar, line column chart. If you have assignment to create a graphical chart from certain data, you could Chart feature in LibreOffice. LibreOffice could possibly present graphical data. It makes you easily analyze data and get trend visually.

This following steps will guide you creating graphical chart in LibreOffice Writer:

1. Firstly, run your LibreOffice Writer.

2. Next, choose **Insert** menu in menu bar then choose **Chart** or you could make it fast by clicking chart button on toolbar. You will be automatically served *a chart wizard.*

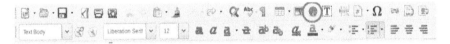

Picture 202: *Button Chart on Toolbar*

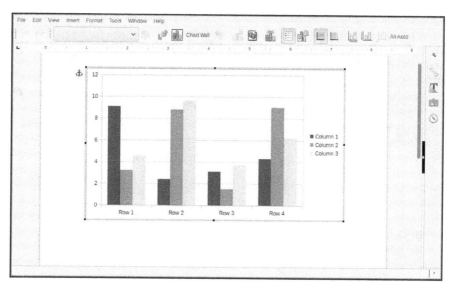

Picture 203: *Chart* preview

2. For instance, we will create graphical data with following information below

Data Pengguna Sistem Operasi PT. Indonesia Merdeka

Nama Sistem Operasi	Tahun 2012	Tahun 2013	Tahun 2014	Tahun 2015
GNU/Linux	54	56	60	80
OSX	70	75	72	94
Windows	144	162	176	215

Table 44: Tabel Data Pengguna Sistem Operasi

3. To transform data into *chart*, choose **View** menu in *menu bar*, then choose **Data Table**, you will be served by *form* such below.

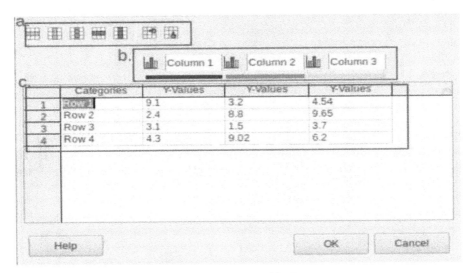

Picture 204: *Data Table* Form

Brief explanation from illustration above:

a) Several option for customizing row.

b) Name from column as reference in creating *chart*.

c) Collection of data for creating *chart*.

4. Next step, you could fulfill certain data from previous table such following illustration below.

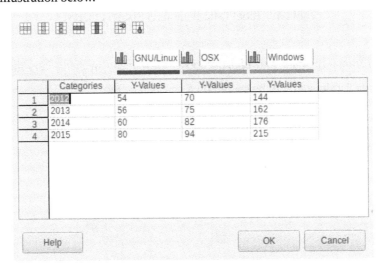

Picture 205: Form Data Table

5. Finally, just click **OK**, you can take following result below.

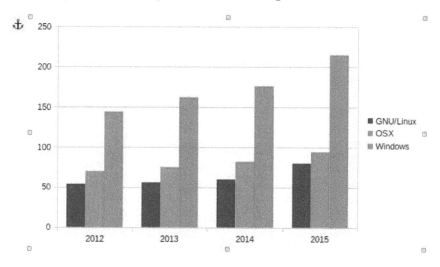

Picture 206: *Chart* preview

6. You could change *chart* type by choosing **Format** in *menu bar* then choose **chart type**.

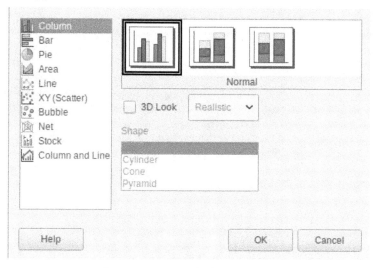

Picture 207: Kind of *Chart* type

7. You can examine variation of interesting *chart* type. For instance, we will implement *chart* with Line style.

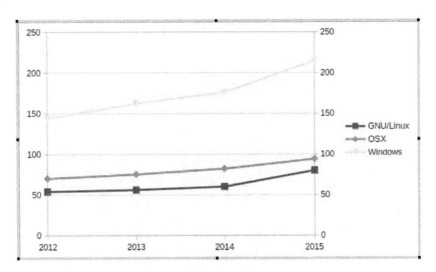

Picture 208: *Chart Line* type

CHANGELOG

This Changelog was written by Taufik Hidayat <<u>yumtaufik1997@gmail.com</u>> as coordinator of Getting Closer With LibreOffice Writer writing project

29 June 2016:

- "Getting Closer With LibreOffice Writer" writing project was started and announced on Telegram group Belajar GNU/Linux Indonesia and Belajar LibreOffice Indonesia.

29 June 2016:

- " Getting Closer With LibreOffice Writer" Changelog was created

16 July 2016 <Rev.1>:

- " Getting Closer With LibreOffice Writer" was started to write.

21 July 2016 <Rev.2>:

- New chapters was added:
  - CHAPTER 1 INTRODUCING TO LIBREOFFICE by Ade Malsasa Akbar <teknoloid@gmail.com>,
  - CHAPTER 2 INTRODUCING TO LIBREOFFICE WRITER INTERFACE by Muhammad Yuga Nugraha <myugan59@gmail.com>,
  - CHAPTER 3 HEADING by Ade Malsasa Akbar <teknoloid@gmail.com>,
  - CHAPTER 4 SHORTCUTS ON LIBREOFFICE WRITER by Ade Malsasa Akbar <teknoloid@gmail.com>,
  - CHAPTER 5 COMPATIBILITY by Mochammad Nur Afandi <muh.afandi.fandi@gmail.com>,
  - CHAPTER 6 HOW TO WRITE ARABIC IN LIBREOFFICE WRITER by Mukafi <kakafi30@gmail.com>,

- CHAPTER 7 CREATING AN AUTOMATIC TABLE OF CONTENT by Taufik Hidayat <yumtaufik1997@gmail.com>,
- CHAPTER 8 PAGE FORMATTING by Anto Samalona <ansamsoftdev@gmail.com>,
- CHAPTER 9 INSERTING PICTURE ON LIBREOFFICE WRITER by Taufik Hidayat <yumtaufik1997@gmail.com>
- CHAPTER 10 CREATING TABLE ON LIBREOFFICE WRITER by Taufik Hidayat <yumtaufik1997@gmail.com>.

22 July 2016 <Rev.3>:
- New chapter was added: CHAPTER 11 SAVING THE DOCUMENT AS A PDF FILE by Taufik Hidayat <yumtaufik1997@gmail.com>.

28 July 2016 <Rev. 4>:
- New chapters was added:
  - CHAPTER 12 INSERTING HEADER AND FOOTER IN LIBREOFFICE WRITER by Sasongko Bawono <sasongko262@gmail.com>, dan
  - CHAPTER 13 SAVING DOCUMENT by Sasongko Bawono <sasongko262@gmail.com>.

04 August 2016 <Rev.5>:
- New chapter was added: CHAPTER 14 MAKINGE LINE SPACING ON LIBREOFFICE WRITER by Taufik Hidayat <yumtaufik1997@gmail.com>.

08 August 2016 <Rev.6>:
- New chapter was added:, CHAPTER 15 FIND AND SMART REPLACE WITH REGULAR EXPRESSION by Ade Malsasa Akbar <teknoloid@gmail.com>.

11 August 2016 <Rev.7>:
- New chapter was added:, CHAPTER 16 INTRODUCING TO LIBREOFFICE
- WRITER SIDEBAR by Mukafi <kakafi30@gmail.com>, dan

- Adding footer Getting Closer With LibreOffice Writer.

12 August 2016 <Rev.7>:

- Restructuring CHAPTERS based on 2, 4, 5, 6 revisions :
  - CHAPTER 1 INTRODUCTION TO LIBREOFFICE by Ade Malsasa Akbar <teknoloid@gmail.com>
  - CHAPTER 2 INTRODUCING TO LIBREOFFICE WRITER INTERFACE by Muhammad Yuga Nugraha <myugan59@gmail.com>
  - CHAPTER 3 HEADING by Ade Malsasa Akbar <teknoloid@gmail.com> was changed to be CHAPTER 5
  - CHAPTER 4 SHORTCUTS ON LIBREOFFICE WRITER by Ade Malsasa Akbar <teknoloid@gmail.com> was changed to be CHAPTER 6
  - CHAPTER 5 COMPATABILITY by Mochammad Nur Afandi <muh.afandi.fandi@gmail.com> was changed to be CHAPTER 7
  - CHAPTER 6 HOW TO WRITE ARABIC IN LIBREOFFICE WRITER by Mukafi <kakafi30@gmail.com> was changed to be CHAPTER 8
  - CHAPTER 7 CREATING AN AUTOMATIC TABLE OF CONTENT by Taufik Hidayat <yumtaufik1997@gmail.com> was changed to be CHAPTER 9
  - CHAPTER 10 PAGE FORMATTING by Anto Samalona <ansamsoftdev@gmail.com>,
  - CHAPTER 11 INSERTING PICTURE ON LIBREOFFICE WRITER by Taufik Hidayat <yumtaufik1997@gmail.com>,
  - CHAPTER 12 CREATING TABLE ON LIBREOFFICE WRITER by Taufik Hidayat <yumtaufik1997@gmail.com>.
  - CHAPTER 16 SIDEBAR by Mukafi <kakafi 30@gmail.com> was changed to be CHAPTER 3
  - CHAPTER 12 INSERTING HEADER AND FOOTER IN LIBREOFFICE WRITER by Sasongko Bawono <sasongko262@gmail.com> was changed to be CHAPTER 14
  - CHAPTER 13 SAVING DOCUMENT by Sasongko Bawono <sasongko262@gmail.com> was changed to be CHAPTER 15

- CHAPTER 14 MAKING LINE SPACING ON LIBREOFFICE WRITER by Taufik Hidayat <yumtaufik1997@gmail.com> was changed to be CHAPTER 16
- CHAPTER 15 FIND AND SMART REPLACE WITH REGULAR EXPRESSION by Ade Malsasa Akbar <teknoloid@gmail.com> was changed to be CHAPTER 17

13 August 2016 <Rev.7.1>:

- Adding new term in technical guide preparation section, it was LibreOffice version which would be used to contribute. It should be in default appearance.

14 August 2016 <Rev.8>:

- Adding new CHAPTER, CHAPTER 17 GETTING FAMILIAR WITH SUB-SUB MENU IN LIBREOFFICE WRITER MENU by Taufik Hidayat <yumtaufik1997@gmail.com>,
- Restructuring CHAPTERS, CHAPTER 17 was changed to be CHAPTER 4 followed by CHAPTER 4 to be CHAPTER 5
- Restructuring the writer's names. They were changed to be the contributors
- Adding editor and cover contributor's name. They are Farah Clara <farah@biawaktamvan.web.id> dan Ade Malsasa Akbar
- Updating number of page target from 100 pages to be 150 pages

19 August 2016 <Rev.8>:

- Adding new CHAPTER, CHAPTER 18 MAIL MERGE IN LIBREOFFICE WRITER by Nur Kholis <khokunsmile@gmail.com>
- Adding new CHAPTER, CHAPTER 19 EYE PROTECTION PAPER IN LIBREOFFICE WRITER by Azis Pratama Akbar <aziz.pratama@gmail.com>.

20 August 2016 <Rev.8>:

- Changing The Contributors section in Editor and Language editor. Editor is Nur Kholis <khokunsmile@gmail.com> and Language Editor is Farah Clara <farah@biawaktamvan.web.id>.

22 August 2016 <Rev.8>:

- Changing Technical Book Preparation section in The number of the book which previously 150 to be 160 pages.

24 August 2016 <Rev.9>:

- Adding new CHAPTER, CHAPTER 20 INTRODUCTION TO GRAPHIC EDITING IN LIBREOFFICE WRITER by Azid <paindustry@yahoo.com>,
- Changing Technical Book Preparation section in The number of the book which previously 160 to be 170 pages.
- Changing several names in CHAPTER 4 in term of Sub-Sub Menu on Menu Bar LibreOffice Writer by Taufik Hidayat <yumtaufik1997@gmail.com> . They were changed to be Menu Bar in LibreOffice Writer.

25 August 2016 <Rev.10>:

- Adding new CHAPTER, CHAPTER 21 INTRODUCING TO OPENDOCUMENT FORMAT by Ade Malsasa Akbar <teknoloid@gmail.com>,
- Changing Technical Book Preparation section in The number of the book which previously 170 to be 180 pages.
- Restructuring CHAPTERS based on 7, 8, 9 revisions:
  - CHAPTER 1 INTRODUCTION TO LIBREOFFICE by Ade Malsasa Akbar <teknoloid@gmail.com>
  - CHAPTER 2 INTRODUCING TO LIBREOFFICE WRITER INTERFACE by Muhammad Yuga Nugraha <myugan59@gmail.com> was changed to be CHAPTER 3
  - CHAPTER 3 SIDEBAR by Mukafi <kakafi 30@gmail.com> was changed to be CHAPTER 4
  - CHAPTER 4 GETTING FAMILIAR WITH SUB-SUB MENU IN LIBREOFFICE WRITER MENU by Taufik Hidayat <yumtaufik1997@gmail.com> was changed to be CHAPTER 5

- CHAPTER 5 HEADING by Ade Malsasa Akbar <teknoloid@gmail.com> was changed to be CHAPTER 6

- CHAPTER 6 SHORTCUTS ON LIBREOFFICE WRITER by Ade Malsasa Akbar <teknoloid@gmail.com> was changed to be CHAPTER 7

- CHAPTER 7 COMPATIBILITY by Mochammad Nur Afandi <muh.afandi.fandi@gmail.com> was changed to be CHAPTER 8

- CHAPTER 8 HOW TO WRITE ARABIC IN LIBREOFFICE WRITER by Mukafi <kakafi30@gmail.com> was changed to be CHAPTER 9

- CHAPTER 9 CREATING AN AUTOMATIC TABLE OF CONTENT by Taufik Hidayat <yumtaufik1997@gmail.com> was changed to be CHAPTER 10

- CHAPTER 10 PAGE FORMATTING by Anto Samalona <ansamsoftdev@gmail.com> was changed to be CHAPTER 11

- CHAPTER 11 tentang Menyisipkan Picture pada LibreOffice Writer oleh Taufik Hidayat <yumtaufik1997@gmail.com> menjadi CHAPTER 12,

- CHAPTER 12 INSERTING PICTURE ON LIBREOFFICE WRITER by Taufik Hidayat <yumtaufik1997@gmail.com> was changed to be CHAPTER 13,

- CHAPTER 13 SAVING THE DOCUMENT AS A PDF FILE by Taufik Hidayat <yumtaufik1997@gmail.com> was changed to be CHAPTER 14

- CHAPTER 14 INSERTING HEADER AND FOOTER IN LIBREOFFICE WRITER by Sasongko Bawono <sasongko262@gmail.com> was changed to be CHAPTER 15

- CHAPTER 15 SAVING DOCUMENT by Sasongko Bawono <sasongko262@gmail.com> was changed to be CHAPTER 16

- CHAPTER 16 MAKING LINE SPACING ON LIBREOFFICE WRITER by Taufik Hidayat <yumtaufik1997@gmail.com> was changed to be CHAPTER 17

- CHAPTER 17 FIND AND SMART REPLACE WITH REGULAR EXPRESSION by Ade Malsasa Akbar <teknoloid@gmail.com> was changed to be CHAPTER 18
- CHAPTER 18 MAIL MERGE IN LIBREOFFICE WRITER by Nur Kholis <khokunsmile@gmail.com> was changed to be CHAPTER 19
- CHAPTER 19 EYE PROTECTION PAPER IN LIBREOFFICE WRITER by Azis Pratama Akbar <aziz.pratama@gmail.com> was changed to be CHAPTER 20
- CHAPTER 20 INTRODUCTION TO GRAPHIC EDITING IN LIBREOFFICE WRITER by Azid <paindustry@yahoo.com> was changed to be CHAPTER 21
- CHAPTER 21 INTRODUCING TO OPENDOCUMENT FORMAT by Ade Malsasa Akbaar <teknoloid@gmail.com> was changed to be CHAPTER 2.

26 August 2016 <Rev.11>:

- Adding new CHAPTER, CHAPTER 22 PRINTING ADDRESS LABELS IN LIBREOFFICE WRITER by Sukamto <kamtono@gmail.com>,
- Changing Technical Book Preparation section in The number of the book which previously 170 to be 200 pages and changing deadline of project from 30 August 2016 to 20 September 2016.

27 August 2016 <Rev.12>:

- Adding new CHAPTER, CHAPTER 23 ARABIC BUCKWALTER CONFIGURATION IN LIBRE OFFICE WRITER by Buono <kangbuono@gmail.com>
- Adding new CHAPTER, CHAPTER 24 LIBREOFFICE MOBILITY by Rahmat Kafabih (Kafabih/KR) <kafalterbang@gmail.com>

28 August 2016 <Rev 13>:

- Adding new CHAPTER, CHAPTER 25 INSERTING MATH FORMULA ON LIBREOFFICE WRITER by Nur Kholis <khokunsmile@gmail.com>

- Adding new CHAPTER, CHAPTER 26 PRINTING DOCUMENTS ON LIBREOFFICE WRITER by Buono <kangbuono@gmail.com>
- Changing Technical Book Preparation section in The number of the book which previously 200 to be 210 pages

01 September 2016 <Rev.14>:

- Adding new CHAPTER, CHAPTER 27 WORKING WITH LIBREOFFICE EXTENSION by Nur Kholis <khokunsmile@gmail.com>,
- Changing Technical Book Preparation section in The number of the book which previously 210 to be 210 pages

12 September 2016 <Rev.15>:

- Changing The Contributors section in adding sub section Language Editor
- Adding new sub CHAPTER sub in CHAPTER 1 by Ade Malsasa Akbar <teknoloid@gmail.com>
- Language editing in CHAPTER 1 by Ahmad Romadhon Hidayatullah <reaamina@gmail.com> dan Ade Malsasa Akbar <teknoloid@gmail.com>
- Language editing in CHAPTER 2 by Ade Malsasa Akbar <teknoloid@gmail.com>

18 September 2016 <Rev.16>:

- Changing The Contributors section in Language editing CHAPTER 21 by Nugroho <nugroho.redbuff@gmail.com>
- Adding new CHAPTER CHAPTER 28 WORKING WITH TRACK CHANGES by Muhammad Irwan Andriawan <andriawan2014@gmail.com>
- Changing Technical Book Preparation section in deadline from 20 September 2016 to be 20 October 2016,
- Changing sub Deadline in Preface in term of deadline from 20 September 2016 to be 30 October 2016.

24 September 2016 <Rev.16>:

- Changing The Contributors section in Language editing CHAPTER 1 until CHAPTER 4 by Faiq Aminuddin <dampuawang@gmail.com>

7 October 2016 <Rev.17>:
- Changing The Contributors section in Language editing CHAPTER 14 by Ahmad Romadhon Hidayatullah <reaamina@gmail.com>
- Changing The Contributors section in Language editing CHAPTER 5 until CHAPTER 7 by Faiq Aminuddin <dampuawang@gmail.com>.

20 October 2016 <Rev.18>:
- Changing The Contributors section in Language editing CHAPTER 7 by Taufik Hidayat <yumtaufik1997@gmail.com>.

23 October 2016 <Rev.19>:
- Changing The Contributors section in Layout editing CHAPTER 5 by Andhika Prasetyo <chupunk3@gmail.com> and CHAPTER 4 by Taufik Hidayat <yumtaufik1997@gmail.com>
- Changing The Contributors section in adding new book editor in sub CHAPTER by Taufik Hidayat <yumtaufik1997@gmail.com> and Abdul Aziz <ingejosmu1048576@gmail.com>,
- Adding new CHAPTER, CHAPTER 29 MAKING CHART IN LIBREOFFICE WRITER by Taufik Mulyana <nothinux.id>

24 October 2016 <Rev.20>:
- Updating Preface in term of cover contributors, Language editor, Book editor and CHAPTER contributors and also promoting the usage of *free software* after Bibliography

29 October 2016 (Rev.20):
- Updating The Contributors section in sub CHAPTER Book editor CHAPTER until CHAPTER 29 by Faiq Aminuddin <dampuawang@gmail.com>,
- Layout editing by Taufik Hidayat <yumtaufik1997@gmail.com>,
- Updating Preface in the number of pages from 219 to be 235 pages.

30 October 2016 (Final):

- Updating book layout by Taufik Hidayat <yumtaufik1997@gmail.com> for mobile version
- Releasing printed ready book by Taufik Hidayat <yumtaufik1997@gmail.com>,
- Releasing mobile version book by Taufik Hidayat <yumtaufik1997@gmail.com>,
- The book was released in 30 October 2016.

TRANSLATION CHANGELOG

This Changelog was written by Muhammad Irwan Andriawan <andriawan2014@gmail.com> as coordinator of Getting Closer With LibreOffice Writer translation project book. The books was translated from Bahasa Indonesia to English. This changelog was made to differ Writing project and Translation project in one book.

28 July 2017:

- Translation project was initiated by Muhammad Irwan Andriawan <andriawan2014@gmail.com> followed by creation of Telegram group "Project Translasi"
- Muhammad Irwan Andriawan <andriawan2014@gmail.com> uploaded the first translation of Preface, The Contributors, Technical Book Preparation sections to the group.

29 July 2017:

- The translated CHAPTER 8 COMPATIBILITY was submitted by Mochammad Nur Afandi <localanu@gmail.com> to Telegram group
- Muhammad Irwan Andriawan reviewed The translated CHAPTER 8 COMPATIBILITY from Mochammad Nur Afandi <localanu@gmail.com>
- Taufik Hidayat <yumtaufik1997@gmail.com> uploaded master file of Getting Closer With LibreOffice Writer book in Bahasa for reference. It would be a reference in translating chapters in English.

31 July 2017:

- The translated CHAPTER 1 INTRODUCTION TO LIBREOFFICE was submitted by Muhammad Fathurridlo <mfathurridlo@gmail.com> to Telegram group

1 August 2017:

- Muhammad Irwan Andriawan <andriawan2014@gmail.com> submitted The translated CHAPTER 28 WORKING WITH TRACK CHANGES to Telegram group

- Muhammad Irwan Andriawan <andriawan2014@gmail.com> reviewed The translated CHAPTER 1 INTRODUCTION TO LIBREOFFICE from Muhammad Fathurridlo <mfathurridlo@gmail.com>

- Muhammad Fathurridlo <mfathurridlo@gmail.com > accepted review The translated CHAPTER 1 INTRODUCTION TO LIBREOFFICE from Muhammad Irwan Andriawan <andriawan2014@gmail.com>

4 August 2017:

- Raymon Rahmadhani <raymon.rahmadhani@gmail.com> submitted The translated CHAPTER 2 INTRODUCING TO OPENDOCUMENT FORMAT to Telegram group

- Muhammad Irwan Andriawan <andriawan2014@gmail.com> reviewed The translated CHAPTER 2 INTRODUCING TO OPENDOCUMENT FORMAT from Raymon Rahmadhani <raymon.rahmadhani@gmail.com>

- Muhammad Fathurridlo <mfathurridlo@gmail.com> submitted The translated CHAPTER 3 INTRODUCING TO LIBREOFFICE WRITER INTERFACE and CHAPTER 4 INTRODUCING TO LIBREOFFICE WRITER SIDEBAR to Telegram group

- Muhammad Irwan Andriawan <andriawan2014@gmail.com> reviewed The translated CHAPTER 3 and CHAPTER 4 from Muhammad Fathurridlo <mfathurridlo@gmail.com>

- Muhammad Irwan Andriawan <andriawan2014@gmail.com> submitted the translated CHAPTER 29 MAKING CHART IN LIBREOFFICE WRITER to Telegram group

- Raymon Rahmadhani <raymon.rahmadhani@gmail.com> reviewed the translated CHAPTER 29 MAKING CHART IN LIBREOFFICE WRITER from Muhammad Irwan Andriawan <andriawan2014@gmail.com>

6 August 2017:

- Ilham Akbar <ilhamsahil05@gmail.com> submitted the translated CHAPTER 6 HEADING to Telegram group

- Muhammad Irwan Andriawan <andriawan2014@gmail.com> reviewed the translated CHAPTER 6 HEADING from Ilham Akbar <ilhamsahil05@gmail.com>

- kucingsebelah <meongpus@hi2.in> submitted the translated CHAPTER 11 PAGE FORMATTING to Telegram group

- Ilham Akbar <ilhamsahil05@gmail.com> submitted the translated CHAPTER 7 SHORTCUTS ON LIBREOFFICE WRITER to Telegram group

- Thoriq Kemal <thoriqcemal@gmail.com> submitted the translated CHAPTER 12 INSERTING PICTURE ON LIBREOFFICE WRITER and CHAPTER 13 CREATING TABLE ON LIBREOFFICE WRITER to Telegram group

- Raymon Rahmadhani <raymon.rahmadhani@gmail.com> accepted feedback from Muhammad Irwan Andriawan <andriawan2014@gmail.com> on The translated CHAPTER 2 INTRODUCING TO OPENDOCUMENT FORMAT to Telegram group

- Muhammad Irwan Andriawan <andriawan2014@gmail.com> submitted the translated CHAPTER 27 WORKING WITH LIBREOFFICE EXTENSION to Telegram group

- <ari> submitted the translated CHAPTER 26 PRINTING DOCUMENTS ON LIBREOFFICE WRITER to Telegram group

- Muhammad Irwan Andriawan <andriawan2014@gmail.com> reviewed the translated CHAPTER 7 SHORTCUTS ON LIBREOFFICE WRITER from Ilham Akbar <ilhamsahil05@gmail.com>

- Muhammad Irwan Andriawan <andriawan2014@gmail.com> reviewed the translated CHAPTER 11 PAGE FORMATTING from kucingsebelah <meongpus@hi2.in>

- Muhammad Fathurridlo <mfathurridlo@gmail.com> was accepted feedback from Muhammad Irwan Andriawan <andriawan2014@gmail.com> on The translated CHAPTER 3 INTRODUCING TO LIBREOFFICE WRITER

INTERFACE and CHAPTER 4 INTRODUCING TO LIBREOFFICE WRITER SIDEBAR

7 August 2017:

- Raymon Rahmadhani <raymon.rahmadhani@gmail.com> submitted The translated CHAPTER 9 HOW TO WRITE ARABIC IN LIBREOFFICE WRITER to Telegram group
- Raymon Rahmadhani <raymon.rahmadhani@gmail.com> submitted The translated CHAPTER 10 CREATING AN AUTOMATIC TABLE OF CONTENT to Telegram group
- Thoriq Kemal <thoriqcemal@gmail.com> submitted the translated CHAPTER 25 INSERTING MATH FORMULA ON LIBREOFFICE WRITER to Telegram group
- Ilham Akbar <ilhamsahil05@gmail.com> submitted the translated CHAPTER 14 SAVING THE DOCUMENT AS A PDF FILE to Telegram group

8 August 2017:

- Muhammad Irwan Andriawan <andriawan2014@gmail.com> reviewed the translated CHAPTER 26 PRINTING DOCUMENTS ON LIBREOFFICE WRITER from <ari>
- Astrida Atni Ayu Mahardini <astriddini7@gmail.com> submitted the translated CHAPTER 5 GETTING ACQUAINTED WITH THE MENU BAR IN LIBREOFFICE WRITER to Telegram group
- Muhammad Irwan Andriawan <andriawan2014@gmail.com> reviewed the translated CHAPTER 10 CREATING AN AUTOMATIC TABLE OF CONTENT from Raymon Rahmadhani <raymon.rahmadhani@gmail.com>
- Muhammad Irwan Andriawan <andriawan2014@gmail.com> reviewed the translated CHAPTER 25 INSERTING MATH FORMULA ON LIBREOFFICE WRITER from Thoriq Kemal <thoriqcemal@gmail.com>

10 August 2017:

- Raymon Rahmadhani <raymon.rahmadhani@gmail.com> submitted revision of the translated CHAPTER 10 CREATING AN AUTOMATIC TABLE OF CONTENT from Raymon Rahmadhani <raymon.rahmadhani@gmail.com> to Telegram group

13 August 2017:

- Muhammad Irwan Andriawan <andriawan2014@gmail.com> reviewed the translated CHAPTER 12 INSERTING PICTURE ON LIBREOFFICE WRITER and CHAPTER 13 CREATING TABLE ON LIBREOFFICE WRITER from Thoriq Kemal <thoriqcemal@gmail.com>
- Muhammad Irwan Andriawan <andriawan2014@gmail.com> reviewed the translated CHAPTER 14 SAVING THE DOCUMENT AS A PDF FILE from Ilham Akbar <ilhamsahil05@gmail.com>
- Muhammad Irwan Andriawan <andriawan2014@gmail.com> reviewed the translated CHAPTER 5 GETTING ACQUAINTED WITH THE MENU BAR IN LIBREOFFICE WRITER from Astrida Atni Ayu Mahardini <astriddini7@gmail.com>

15 August 2017:

- Muhammad Irwan Andriawan <andriawan2014@gmail.com> submitted the translated CHAPTER 24 LIBREOFFICE MOBILITY to Telegram group

20 August 2017:

- Astrida Atni Ayu Mahardini <astriddini7@gmail.com> submitted the translated CHAPTER 17 MAKING LINE SPACING ON LIBREOFFICE WRITER and CHAPTER 18 FIND AND SMART REPLACE WITH REGULAR EXPRESSION to Telegram group

21 August 2017:

- Muhammad Irwan Andriawan <andriawan2014@gmail.com> reviewed the translated CHAPTER 17 MAKING LINE SPACING ON LIBREOFFICE WRITER from Astrida Atni Ayu Mahardini <astriddini7@gmail.com>

- Azis R. Pratama <azis.pratama@gmail.com> submitted the translated CHAPTER 20 EYE PROTECTION PAPER IN LIBREOFFICE WRITER to Telegram group

22 August 2017:

- Muhammad Irwan Andriawan <andriawan2014@gmail.com> reviewed the translated CHAPTER 18 FIND AND SMART REPLACE WITH REGULAR EXPRESSION from Astrida Atni Ayu Mahardini <astriddini7@gmail.com>
- Muhammad Irwan Andriawan <andriawan2014@gmail.com> reviewed the translated CHAPTER 20 EYE PROTECTION PAPER IN LIBREOFFICE WRITER from Azis R. Pratama <azis.pratama@gmail.com>

25 August 2017:

- Azis R. Pratama <azis.pratama@gmail.com> submitted the translated CHAPTER 23 ARABIC BUCKWALTER CONFIGURATION IN LIBRE OFFICE WRITER to Telegram group

27 August 2017:

- kucingsebelah <meongpus@hi2.in> submitted the translated CHAPTER 16 SAVING DOCUMENT to Telegram group

29 August 2017:

- Faiq Aminuddin <faiq.aminuddin.demak@gmail.com> submitted the translated CHAPTER 15 INSERTING HEADER AND FOOTER IN LIBREOFFICE WRITER to Muhammad Irwan Andriawan <andriawan2014@gmail.com>

1 September 2017:

- Astrida Atni Ayu Mahardini <astriddini7@gmail.com> submitted the translated CHAPTER 19 MAIL MERGE IN LIBREOFFICE WRITER and

CHAPTER 22 PRINTING ADDRESS LABELS IN LIBREOFFICE WRITER
to Telegram group

3 September 2017:

- Muhammad Irwan Andriawan <andriawan2014@gmail.com> reviewed the translated CHAPTER 16 SAVING DOCUMENT from kucingsebelah <meongpus@hi2.in>

- Muhammad Irwan Andriawan <andriawan2014@gmail.com> reviewed the translated CHAPTER 15 INSERTING HEADER AND FOOTER IN LIBREOFFICE WRITER from Faiq Aminuddin <faiq.aminuddin.demak@gmail.com>

- Muhammad Irwan Andriawan <andriawan2014@gmail.com> reviewed the translated CHAPTER 23 ARABIC BUCKWALTER CONFIGURATION IN LIBRE OFFICE WRITER from Azis R. Pratama <azis.pratama@gmail.com>

- Muhammad Irwan Andriawan <andriawan2014@gmail.com> reviewed the translated CHAPTER 22 PRINTING ADDRESS LABELS IN LIBREOFFICE WRITER from Astrida Atni Ayu Mahardini <astriddini7@gmail.com>

- Muhammad Irwan Andriawan <andriawan2014@gmail.com> reviewed the translated CHAPTER 19 MAIL MERGE IN LIBREOFFICE WRITER from Astrida Atni Ayu Mahardini <astriddini7@gmail.com>

20 September 2017:

- Risma Fahrul Amin <rismafahrulamin@gmail.com> submitted the translated CHAPTER 21 INTRODUCING TO GRAPHIC IN LIBREOFFICE WRITER to Muhammad Irwan Andriawan <andriawan2014@gmail.com>

20 October 2017:

- Muhammad Irwan Andriawan <andriawan2014@gmail.com> changed original cover of the book

2 November 2017:

- Muhammad Irwan Andriawan <andriawan2014@gmail.com> released the final translated book